TEN MASTER HISTORIANS

To the memory of
my Mother,
descended from the
Earls of Angus,
who have for so long
played a valiant part
in the history of
Scotland

DAVID HUME

The great philosopher and premier Scottish historian

Ten
Master Historians

by

LIONEL MILNER ANGUS-BUTTERWORTH

Essay Index Reprint Series

BOOKS FOR LIBRARIES PRESS
FREEPORT, NEW YORK

© L. M. Angus-Butterworth 1961
First published 1961 by Aberdeen University Press
Second edition Aberdeen University Press 1962
Reprinted 1969 by arrangement with the publisher

STANDARD BOOK NUMBER:
8369-0000-6

LIBRARY OF CONGRESS CATALOG CARD NUMBER:
69-18919

PRINTED IN THE UNITED STATES OF AMERICA

Contents

Illustrations

Introduction

It will be found that some challenging views have been expressed about the historians considered here. Adam Smith was such an original thinker and innovator that he was not regarded as a historian at the time he wrote, largely because his interests were outside the narrow limits of what was then accepted as history. But the development of economic history as a major branch of historical study now gives him the right to be classed as a master historian. Goldsmith is so well-known as a writer of supreme genius in other fields that his eminence as a historian has long been obscured. Yet he is entitled to rank as the senior English (as opposed to Scottish) historian of the modern period, and therefore became a natural choice for the present work. It appears that this is the first time he has been considered solely as a historian.

While giving recognition to Adam Smith and Goldsmith, and according fuller appreciation than has been customary to comparatively neglected historians like Froude, it has, on the other hand, been found desirable to reassess in some cases men who have stood unduly high in the public estimation. Macaulay, who imposed himself so successfully on his contemporaries, has already been the subject of severe criticism by others, although only now is it becoming evident just how commonplace his mind was. Gibbon, in contrast, has kept his reputation longer, but the time is ripe for making a fresh estimate of him.

Even leading historians naturally vary a good deal in status. Although Southey is not so outstanding as some, his inclusion here is justified by his work in the special field of Brazilian history, which has remained exclusively his own, while his pleasing personality is an additional if lesser reason for finding him a congenial object of study. And new stars do sometimes appear in the firmament, albeit at long intervals. Churchill has so recently joined the ranks of the master historians that, although general biographies of him have frequently been published, there has been no monograph devoted to his historical work.

The chief historians often appear to have been keenly critical of conventional theology. Some of the early ones, like Hume and Gibbon, were circumspect in their dealings with the ecclesiastical hierarchy, but were nevertheless made to feel the animosity of the Church. Of the later ones Froude and Green were unwary, and the former in particular was made to suffer most unjustly in consequence. It is not a little remarkable that men with strongly marked personalities and idiosyncrasies, separated by long distances of time and circumstance, should be so unanimous in their broad rationalistic outlook.

It was not possible within the scope of the present book to include all the English-speaking historians who have secured fame. To have added others would have been pleasant, but those chosen seemed to have the best claims on a variety of grounds —the quality of their work, the interest of their careers, the soundness of their views, and their personal attributes. The aim throughout has been to consider the man as well as his work: to see why he wrote history and how he set about it. The task has been a fascinating one.

L. M. ANGUS-BUTTERWORTH

ASHTON NEW HALL,
ASHTON-ON-MERSEY,
CHESHIRE

CHAPTER I

The Changing Conception Of History

WHILE it is evident that the modern conception of history is far removed from the kind of record made by the early English and French chroniclers, there can be no doubt that the work of the "historians" of antiquity is vastly more remote again. If we consider, for example, the Greek writers in this field, we find that their limitations were extreme. Thucydides took the Peloponnesian war for his subject and excluded everything else. J. B. Bury says of Xenophon that his mind was essentially mediocre, and incapable of penetrating beneath the surface of things. But the essence of the matter is expressed by the American authoress Miss Bessie Graham, when she says of Herodotus that, "He had no conception of the modern idea of investigating sources and evidence. The study of archaeology was unknown, so he relied on folk tales and early poetic accounts, and adapted what he heard or read to his own interpretation. The histories form a story book, written in the style of artless conversation." Primitive conditions caused a broad comprehensive outlook to be lacking, for the rich scope and global range of modern knowledge were absent. Resources of learning which we now accept as normal were then non-existent.

Chroniclers fulfilled an essential historical function in recording important events in which they had taken part or about which they had heard from eye-witnesses. They were among the forerunners of historians, but the conception is a very different one, and we can trace a distinct evolution from them. There are few more fascinating figures than Sir John Froissart, of the latter part of the fourteenth and early part of the fifteenth centuries: the value of his work is immense, yet we cannot regard him as other than purely a chronicler. By the seventeenth century we have in Clarendon the chronicler-historian, who retains many of the characteristics of the old type of chronicler while going some way towards meeting the exacting demands now made upon the historian. Even in the twentieth

century a worthy element of the chronicler tradition survives in
Churchill, but he is nevertheless a true historian in that, although he deals with events of which he has personal knowledge,
he uses with consummate skill all the world-wide sources through
which today information can be checked and counter-checked to
ensure the highest possible standard of accuracy; he gives full
evidence for his statements in the form of very complete docu-
mentation, derived from home, allied and enemy records; and
he has the vision and the grand impartiality of one exceptionally well fitted by temperament to write for posterity.

In recording the past, two main processes are involved.
There is first the ascertaining of facts, which can usually best be
done by scientific methods. Then follows the need for presenting in literary form the information obtained, which is more of
an artistic matter. Thus history may be regarded as a combination of science and art. It is, however, necessary to have in mind
the qualification that, as history has to cover all the infinitely
variable factors affecting human life, it can never be part of an
exact science. We have also to notice that the proportions
of the two elements are not stable, and that for some time
past historians have increasingly stressed the need for scientific
accuracy in their researches.

In early historical works there was a substantial admixture
of romance. The critical spirit was not yet awake, and folklore
and legend were given at least as much prominence as more
sober features. Prejudice, too, was often apparent. The resulting narrative, however, if unreliable as evidence, was frequently
picturesque and colourful, so that a great deal of pleasure was
derived from it as a branch of literature. We have now moved
so far in the opposite direction that upon occasion the results of
historical research are presented in the very forbidding form of
a collection of facts and data that appear not only dull and
wearisome, but trivial and unrelated. And, of course, historians
with no particular literary gift are inclined to look with a
jaundiced eye upon those who have, and to suspect that work
is unsound if it is well written.

A warning against the writing of historical abstractions is
given by Professor Wilbur Cortez Abbott of Harvard, the doyen
of American historians. "It was men who made history," he
says, "and the greatest of historians have been the most human."

Elsewhere he writes: "History is no mere accumulation of facts; it is not masses of notes and information; it is not the product of a 'lifetime of horrid industry' alone. It requires more than the ability to read endless volumes and manuscripts and make endless references. It requires thought. It needs the mind as well as the eye and hand. Without thought it is but sounding brass and tinkling cymbal, out of tune and harsh. Without informing ideas it becomes a chaos void and without form."

It is possible to observe changes not only in what is regarded as appropriate subject-matter for history, but in the language used. A classical bias was long evident, but a freer style was gradually achieved. Thus Professor Legouis says of Clarendon's *History of the Rebellion and Civil Wars in England*: "It is traditional in form; the long sentences are indefinite in outline; the passage from the Latin period to the short and concise modern style is in progress but is not yet achieved. From this results a certain awkwardness." In actual fact it was not until much later that it became possible to escape more completely from this tyranny. Gibbon's preference for words of Latin origin is evident, and like Macaulay, who shares this feature, he is given to rhetorical and grandiloquent phrasing which to present taste has come to seem unpleasantly pompous. Carlyle, too, found himself so inextricably enmeshed in a hideously barbarous and curiously tortured style of no known lineage that he had the greatest difficulty in expressing himself. In the last hundred years, however, the native vigour of Anglo-Saxon wording has come into its own with Froude and Green, while Churchill's affinity to Defoe is very close.

Related to the question of how far history is an art, and how far a science, is the feature that the great historians have not been professionals. They have devoted themselves naturally to historical research and the writing of history in mature life, although even then combined with other occupations, but their education, their training and their intentions in the early part of their careers were towards quite other objectives. There is a parallel here to creative work in other branches of literature: the great playwright, poet or novelist is not trained to that end. Probably the root of the matter is that what is really being studied is life itself in its wider manifestations: the historian like the novelist must understand humanity, and must have experience of men's motives. There needs to be interpretation of events through sympathetic insight. In this there is surely more of art than of science. It is even conceivable that the potentially good historian might be converted into a mediocre one by imposing too much formal education.

There is one exception to the above reasoning which is of rapidly increasing consequence. Economic history is much more of a science than general history, and different conditions therefore apply to it: unlike the older branches of the subject it has from the beginning been the preserve of academic investigators. The opportunities for research, with so much virgin land available, have been immense, and have been seized with ardour. Seldom can scholars have had such rich territory to explore and survey. Those so ably engaged in this work have nearly all been senior members of the staffs of the universities.

In the past the study of history has been devoted too exclusively to certain branches of the subject, namely to Regal, Martial and Ecclesiastical History. Largely within the last fifty years, however, there has been a striking change of emphasis. The growth of democracy has caused the history of royalty, with its petty dynastic problems and its accounts of the personal actions of monarchs, to develop into Political History, covering the whole organization of government, in both its constitutional and administrative aspects. The history of military matters has become a specialized study, sometimes highly technical, and, being the branch that is concerned mainly with wars, we may hope that in future generations, when mankind has become more civilized, it may become entirely obsolete. We are even beginning to get vivid glimpses of the life of our very remote ancestors, engaged in their gallant struggle with the forces of nature before the dawn of history, from such works as the late Professor V. Gordon Childe's *Prehistory of Scotland*.

The great developments in the present century have been in Economic and Social History. It is almost incredible that these aspects, which are so absorbingly interesting and so vitally important, should have been neglected for so long. The distinction between the two is not sharply defined. In Adam Smith's magnificent tapestry both elements are inextricably interwoven and, although he is regarded as primarily an economic historian, his uncanny insight into social history is manifest: he is, indeed, the forerunner of all who since his day have come to carry forward and extend his work.

The range of what has been accomplished in these newer branches in recent years is remarkable. On the economic side we have the *Cambridge Economic History of Europe from the Decline of the Roman Empire,* by Professor Sir John Clapham and Dr. Eileen Power. Clapham also wrote an *Economic History of Modern Britain,* and Professor E. Lipson an *Economic History of England.* Professor T. S. Ashton has contributed a brilliant short work on *The Industrial Revolution, 1760-1830,* admirable alike for its distinguished scholarship and for its beautiful English. Complementary to these are such studies as Jevons's *British Coal Trade;* Ashton's *Iron and Steel in the Industrial Revolution;* Daniels's *Early English Cotton Industry;* and Lipson's *History of the Woollen and Worsted Industries.* On the social side we have the *English Social History* by G. M. Trevelyan, and such specialized works as Redford's *History of Local Government in Manchester.* The preoccupation with this kind of work has been so complete that there has been a significant paucity of general historians, Churchill being the only important example in the present century.

A very interesting change of attitude in connection with the writing and teaching of history can be traced in a growing sense of moral responsibility as regards the interpretation of historical facts. Perhaps the first evidence of this is to be found in a recommendation, of a Universal Peace Conference held in 1889, that the amount of space devoted to wars in history textbooks should be reduced. Wider in scope was the action taken by the Norden Association in Sweden, Denmark, Finland and Iceland in 1919, when the experts examined one hundred and twenty-six books used in teaching history in Scandinavian countries, considered the way in which controversial questions were treated, and recommended fair comment and more information on neighbouring countries.

In July 1950, the Brunswick group of historians, under the leadership of Professor Dr. Eckert, met a group of six British history teachers and university lecturers to try to reach agreement on certain controversial points of German and British history between 1890 and 1914. Again in August of the same year Unesco (United Nations Educational, Scientific and Cultural Organization) organized an International Educational Seminar in Brussels at which the treatment of local, national and world history was studied, with a view to determining what information was likely to promote international understanding. The need for the integration of national into international history was recognized.

The value of such discussions may be great if there is frankness and a genuine desire on the part of all those concerned to reach the truth. There can, for example, be ample scope for legitimate pride in real national achievements, while unqualified condemnation is given to the deliberate corruption of history to deceive students and the public for political ends. It is, in fact, becoming ever more essential for the historian to shed any petty parochial prejudices and to maintain a strictly cosmopolitan impartiality.

CHAPTER II

David Hume

(1711-1776)

In the writing of history, there is a need for wide knowledge and experience of men and affairs. Without an adequate background of this kind the task of interpreting the thoughts and actions of past generations would appear to offer insuperable difficulties. David Hume, before turning to history in full maturity and at the height of his powers, had already had a distinguished career in other fields. Professor Emile Legouis of the Sorbonne accurately terms him the greatest European philosopher of the important middle period of the eighteenth century. Hill Burton shows that his philosophy had such outstanding quality, and such freshness and decision, that "he set a whole army of philosophers at work, either to refute what he had said, or seriously to fill up the blanks which he discovered".

The ancestry of Hume is notable. He was descended from a cadet branch of the family of the Earls of Home. He remarks that "the practice of spelling the name Hume is by far the most ancient and most general till about the Restoration, when it became common to spell it Home, contrary to pronunciation".

Among the historian's earlier kinsmen were many men of marked distinction. Thus Sir Alexander Home was Ambassador to England in 1450. David Hume (c. 1560-c. 1630), second son of Sir David Hume of Wedderburn, became in 1583 private secretary to his relation Archibald, eighth Earl of Angus, and was later the author of *A General History of Scotland*. Another kinsman was Sir David Hume (1643-1707), appointed a Scottish judge in 1689, and afterwards one of the senators of the College of Justice in Edinburgh. The historian's own nephew, Professor David Hume (1757-1838), held the chair of Scots Law in the University of Edinburgh.

It is evident that Hume felt justifiable pride in coming of good stock, for he writes: "I am not of the opinion of some, that these matters are altogether to be slighted. Though we should pretend to be wiser than our ancestors, yet it is arrogant to pretend that we are wiser than the other nations of Europe who, all of them except perhaps the English, make great account of their family descent. I doubt that our morals have not much improved since we began to think riches the sole thing worth regarding."

Hume's father was Laird of the estate of Ninewells in Berwickshire. The family mansion stood on an eminence, with fine timber on either side. In front was a gentle declivity with the river Whitadder running at its foot. The picturesque name of the property was taken from a cluster of nine springs which rose on this slope. Included in the coat of arms of this branch of the family were "nine wells, or springs, barry-wavy and argent".

David Hume was born in his father's town house in Edinburgh on 26 April 1711. He was a younger son, and as such had to make his own way in the world, for the landed estate passed to his elder brother. He remarks: "My family was not rich, and being myself a younger brother my patrimony, according to the mode of my country, was of course very slender. My father, who passed for a man of parts, died when I was an infant leaving me, with an elder brother and sister, under the care of our mother, a woman of singular merit, who, though young and handsome, devoted herself entirely to the rearing and education of her children."

Hume attended the University of Edinburgh and afterwards studied law. In April 1730, when he was just nineteen years of age, he suffered from a breakdown in health caused by having applied himself too closely to his studies. As regards his mental work, he says that "all my ardour seemed in a moment to be extinguished, and I could no longer raise my mind to that pitch which formerly gave me such excessive pleasure". His physician warned him against overwork, and Hume says: "I now began to take some indulgence to myself; studied moderately, leaving off before I was weary. Upon his (the doctor's) advice I drank an English pint of claret wine every day, and rode eight or ten Scotch miles. There grew upon me a ravenous appetite and as quick a digestion. This appetite nourished me extremely, so that from being tall, lean and raw-boned I became the most sturdy, robust, healthful-like fellow you have seen, with a ruddy complexion and a cheerful countenance."

When he was twenty-three Hume went to live in France. His father being dead he had to live on the slender patrimony of £50 a year, and the cost of living was low on the Continent. He records that, "I went over to France with a view of prosecuting my studies in a country retreat; and I there laid that plan of life which I have steadily and successfully pursued. I resolved to make a very rigid frugality supply my deficiency of fortune, to maintain unimpaired my independency, and to regard every object as contemptible except the improvement of my talent in literature." He lived very agreeably in France for three years, first for a short time in Paris, then at Rheims, and finally for a long spell at La Flèche. He returned in 1738 upon completing his famous *Treatise of Human Nature*. The Treatise met at first with a very cold reception, failing even to excite a murmur among the zealots. But David, being naturally of a cheerful and sanguine temper, was not discouraged, and continued his studies with enthusiasm.

While in France the future historian and philosopher pursued his literary studies in strict retirement, reading widely in English, French, Italian and Latin. He brought back with him not only an intimate knowledge of the French people and their language, which was to stand him in good stead on a number of occasions later, but a matured cosmopolitan outlook. He had learnt also to cultivate a philosophic outlook in his own life.

In 1741-42 Hume produced two volumes of *Essays, Moral and Philosophical*, some of them remarkable for research, originality and elegance of style. In 1744 he became a candidate for the Chair of Moral Philosophy in the Edinburgh University. He received influential support but failed to secure the appointment because the clergy and some others raised determined opposition on account of the outspoken character of his philosophical writings. In the course of a letter to a friend, written at this time, he says: "I am informed that popular clamour has been raised against me in Edinburgh on account of scepticism, heterodoxy and other hard names, which confound the ignorant." From the beginning of his career he maintained a fixed resolution not to reply to criticism of his work, and with his good humoured tolerance easily kept clear of all literary squabbles.

The prejudice which Hume had to face was in a sense a tribute to his advanced thought. He had established himself as a philosopher of the highest rank in a period notable for rationalistic investigations that were hampered by the resistance of the religious-minded. Legouis observes that Hume analyzed more boldly than Locke the elements of knowledge, and that he bordered on complete scepticism; although less aggressive than the French *philosophes,* he was not less hostile to Christianity. Unlike many later philosophers, who appear to regard obscurity as a merit, "nothing could be more tranquil and assured than the march of his thought, nothing clearer than the prose in which he pursued his most subtle analyses in lucid and sober language".

Early in 1746 Hume was invited by General St. Clair to attend him as secretary in a campaign against the French. The General also appointed him Judge Advocate of all the forces under his command by a commission "given on board His Majesty's ship *Superb* the third day of August, 1746". The choice was a very happy one. Hill Burton observes that the mixed ministerial and judicial duties of a judge advocate require a general knowledge of the great principles of law and justice, with a freedom from that technical thraldom of the practical lawyer which would be unsuitable to the rapidity of military operations; and there can be little doubt that these delicate and important functions were, in this instance, committed to one in every way capable of performing them in a satisfactory manner. And Hume was adequately rewarded for his services, for when writing to his kinsman "Mr. Alexander Home, Advocate, His Majesty's Solicitor for Scotland, at Edinburgh," he says: "As to myself, my way of life is agreeable; and though it may not be so profitable as I am told, yet so large an army as will be under the general's command must certainly render my perquisites very considerable."

The expedition sailed from Plymouth, and an attack by land and sea forces was made upon Port L'Orient, then a fine town on the coast of Brittany and the seat of the French East India trade. The place proved too strong to be taken. Later, possession was taken of the peninsula of Quiberon, as also of the two islands of Houat and Hedia. Thus Hume was among those historians who, in writing of warfare, described a science of which they had had practical experience.

At the close of the campaign Hume returned to Ninewells, but soon afterwards St. Clair, who had come to hold him in the highest esteem, persuaded the historian to accompany him on a military embassy to Vienna, and in 1748 to Turin. He came back with increased experience, and "master of near a thousand pounds".

Although the mission to Turin was destined to make Hume independent, he himself felt reluctance to leave his books and the leisure of his retreat. Once he had set out, however, he kept an entertaining and instructive journal of his adventures for the amusement of his family at home. On the outward journey he spent some time in Holland, in March, and found it "in all its native deformity". He declared that "nothing can be more disagreeable than that heap of dirt and mud and ditches and reeds which they here call a country". He adds that he had understood that in Holland the land and water, after many struggles to see which should be master, had at last agreed to share it between them; but that in fact the land had come by much the worst bargain, and had much the smaller share of the possession.

Travelling was far from comfortable. After leaving Coblentz he remarks that: "The road is disagreeable for a coach; sometimes you go along the side of a hill with a precipice below you, and have not an inch to spare; and the road hanging all the way towards the precipice, so that one had need to have a good head to look out of the windows."

But the historian found keen pleasure in observation, writing that: "There are great advantages in travelling, and nothing serves more to remove prejudices." He had not had a favourable impression of Germany in advance, but admired much of what he saw there. He says, for example: "We were all very much taken up with the town of Nurenberg, where we lay two nights ago; the houses, though old-fashioned, and of a grotesque figure (having sometimes five or six stories of garrets), yet are they solid, well built, complete and cleanly. The people are handsome, well clothed and well fed; an air of industry and contentment, without splendour, prevails through the whole."

At Vienna the British ambassador presented Hume and his party at court. The historian records that, "after we had had a little conversation with Her Imperial Majesty, we were to walk backwards through a very long room, curtsying all the way, and there was very great danger of our falling foul of each other, as well as of tumbling topsy-turvy. She saw the difficulty we were in and immediately called to us, 'Allez, allez, Messieurs, sans cérémonie. Vous n'êtes pas accoutumés à ce mouvement, et le plancher est glissant.' We esteemed ourselves very much obliged to her for this attention, especially my companions, who were desperately afraid of my falling on them and crushing them."

When in 1751 his elder brother married, David Hume had already made considerable progress in establishing himself, and arranged that he and his sister should leave the family roof. In this connection he writes to a relation: "Since my brother's departure (to his wedding), Kathy and I have been computing in our turn, and the result of our deliberation is that we are to take up house. If arithmetic and frugality don't deceive us (and they are pretty certain arts) we shall be able, after providing for hunger, warmth and cleanliness, to keep a stock in reserve." In addition to his own modest income his sister had £30 a year and "an equal love of order and frugality". David was already beginning to grow corpulent, and closes the letter quoted with this whimsical message to his kinsman the Solicitor-General for Scotland: "My compliments to His Solicitorship. Unfortunately, I have not a horse at present to carry my fat carcass to pay its respects to his superior obesity."

Hume and his sister settled in Edinburgh. He therefore moved "from the country to the town, the true scene for a man of letters". A few months after his arrival in the Scottish capital he was made Keeper of the Library of the Faculty of Advocates in Edinburgh, which has since become the National Library of Scotland. The salary was only £40 a year, but the library was the largest in Scotland and contained a good collection of British history. He could accordingly devote himself to his "historical projects". Before turning to historical work, however, he had completed his *Political Discourses*, which were published in 1752.

The *Discourses* were translated into French by the Abbé Le Blanc in 1754, and passed through several editions. Sir Leslie Stephen says that Hume became an authority in France, where the rising school of economists was stimulated by his clear and original expositions. Professor C. R. Fay, the economist, speaks of the great friendship between Hume and Adam Smith, which remained unbroken on such ideal lines until the death of the former. In referring to Adam Smith he says: "With David Hume, his life-long friend, he shared the give and take of intellectual friendship. If priority of publication is to decide, then it was Hume's *Essay on the Balance of Trade* in 1752 which first exposed the essential fallacies in the balance of trade argument." It was in September, 1752, that Hume informed Adam Smith, already his closest friend, that he had begun his historical research "with great ardour and pleasure". About the same time, he wrote to another friend, Dr. Clephane: "As there is no happiness without occupation, I have begun a work which will employ me several years, and which yields me much satisfaction. 'Tis a History of Britain."

The kindly nature of David Hume caused him to show prompt and practical sympathy when he met with any genuine example of distress or misfortune. One striking instance of this is found in his connection with the blind poet Blacklock. Soon after Hume had begun his historical work, and was devoting his energies very fully to it, he became aware that Blacklock, a man of gentle and sensitive character, was trying to rear a large family in spite of the most extreme poverty. The historian, who had not yet had time to proceed far with his history, immediately broke off his own work to conduct a campaign on behalf of the poet, for whom he found a publisher and friends who were prepared to give assistance. And after publication of the poems he wrote to Professor John Stewart of the Edinburgh University: "I hope you are very zealous in promoting the sale of Blacklock's poems. I will never be reconciled to you unless you can dispose of at least a score of them; and make your friends Sir John Maxwell and Lord Buchan pay a guinea apiece for their copy."

The help thus begun was continued firmly. An opportunity of extending it came about in a curious way. As Librarian of the Faculty of Advocates it was Hume's duty to purchase new works. His special interest in, and knowledge of, French literature caused him to introduce works by important authors like Crébillon and La Fontaine. In an amazing exhibition of narrow-minded prejudice and ignorance, Sir David Dalrymple and

Mr. James Burnet, curators of the library, when checking the accounts of new purchases, ordered that these books, including La Fontaine's Fables, should be struck out of the catalogue and removed from the shelves as indecent books, unworthy of a place in a learned library. Hume was angry, and while he determined to remain as librarian because of the facilities it gave him for historical research, he resolved that in future he would accept no salary for the duties he undertook. He accordingly made formal arrangements for the salary to be paid to Blacklock, although he himself continued to do all the work. In a note to Adam Smith he says: "Being equally unwilling to lose the use of the books and to bear an indignity, I retain the office but have given Blacklock, our blind poet, a bond of annuity for the salary. I have now put it out of these malicious fellows' power to offer me any indignity, while my motive for remaining in this office is so apparent."

This incident of Blacklock and the Advocates' Library indicates not only the generosity of the historian but his hardy and resolute temper. He cultivated increasingly a calm and un-impassioned outlook, but while he conquered any outward demonstration of strong feeling, even in later years his force of character was only regulated and not extinguished.

What Hume wrote was subject to minute and rigorous correction. Sometimes, when he had written a passage, he would cross it out and substitute another; then, on comparing the two, he would restore the original wording; and finally, upon thinking of some happier phrasing, he would make a further change. While he was always prepared to take trouble in this way, it is noteworthy that some of his most brilliant passages show hardly any sign of alteration. He had a real feeling for the use of words, and constantly substituted shorter and more familiar ones for those he had used to begin with. We find, for example, the phrase "His dignity was exempted from pride" altered in a second edition to "His dignity was free from pride", and "effectuate a marriage" changed to "effect a marriage". Easier phrasing also received attention, as when "under pretext of a hunting match" became "on pretence of a hunting match", and "to those effects which were operated" became "to those effects which were wrought". Here, as elsewhere, the aim of the historian was to fulfil the Duke of Buckingham's definition of fine writing—"exact propriety of words and thought". It is rare for compositions to meet these conditions successfully, but Hume's virile energy enabled him to maintain a consistently high standard in his literary work.

As his work progressed, he was obliged to extend his sources of reference in various ways. He employed agents to obtain books for him and, in the proper spirit of the frugal Scot, sold the volume when he could to the Advocates' library, as appears from the following extract from a letter to Andrew Millar: "I am very busy, and am making some progress; but find that this part of English history is a work of infinite labour and study, which, however, I do not grudge; for I have nothing better nor more agreeable to employ me. I have sent you a short catalogue of books, which either are not in the Advocates' library or are not to be found at present. I must beg of you to procure them for me and to send them down with the first ship. Send me also the prices; for I shall be able to engage the curators of the library to take from me such as they want at the price." Again, in dealing with another section of his history he writes: "I find the Advocates' library very well provided with books in this period: but before I finish I shall pass a considerable time in London to peruse the manuscripts in the Museum." When, at a later stage, he began to think of dates of publication, he felt that he could make no fixed plans, because the quality of his work had to take first place. He remarked, "This is not a matter which I can hurry on faster than I am able to satisfy myself in the execution."

The first volume of Hume's history, dealing with the reigns of Charles I and James I, was published at the end of 1754. This volume alone brought him nearly £2,000. A second volume carried the history to the Revolution of 1688. Working backwards, he published in 1759 two volumes containing the history of the house of Tudor. In 1761 there appeared the two final volumes, dealing with the period from Julius Caesar to Henry VII. The financial return grew as the work progressed. Hume's historical writings came to succeed so well that his "copy-money" exceeded anything previously known in England. The historian became "not only independent but opulent". With enlarged means he could consider a change in his somewhat austere mode of life, and with this object in view he sought a new residence.

In May 1762, Hume removed to James's Court in the Lawn-market. This kind of square or closed court was a device used in the Scottish metropolis, as by the old French nobility, to secure for a small community not only privacy but better light-ing and greater cleanliness than could be provided for the in-habitants at large. Hume's house was on a hillside, and looked out over the North Loch, then a lake that came within a few yards of the base of the building. Beyond the water of the loch lay land on which are now the streets and squares of the New Town, but which was then woodland, open heath or agricultural ground. The historian-philosopher could therefore hardly have chosen a pleasanter prospect.

In estimating the value of Hume's history, Burton says that the historian was the first to add to a mere narrative of events an enquiry into the progress of the people and of their arts, literature, manners and general social condition. This under-taking was then a very original one, and in brief consisted of widening the scope of historical work by adding a study of the social and economic conditions of the time to purely political history. Further, as Sir Leslie Stephen remarks, Hume's literary ability made the book incomparably superior to the diluted party pamphlets or painful compilations that had hitherto passed for history.

Hume's style excels in both dignity and clarity. One feels that he is grandly impartial and disinterested, so that an admir-able sense of proportion is evident. His work became the standard history of England, and long maintained that position. Not only has his history high literary merit, so that it can be read today with undiminished pleasure, but his views upon men and events remain well in accordance with modern thought and knowledge. Dr. Sampson suggests that, because his history was so well written, historians who could not write declared it unsound, but that it still retains importance as the first large-scale history of England to attain high rank as a literary com-position.

When the historian moved to James's Court he set up a chaise and arranged everything comfortably with a view to permanent settlement in Edinburgh. At the same time he retained some close contacts with France. The Comtesse de Boufflers had entered into a correspondence with him, which led later to a confidential friendship. Lord Elibank told him at this time that no living author had ever enjoyed such a reputation as he now possessed in Paris. So it came about that he was invited to accompany the Marquis of Hertford when the latter was appointed Ambassador at Paris after the peace of 1763.

Hume arrived in France in October 1763, and was received with extraordinary enthusiasm. Literary eminence in Paris was a passport to the most exclusive society, and he was warmly received by the royal family. On his first appearance at Court the children of the Dauphin, the future Louis XVI, Louis XVIII and Charles X, then aged nine to six, had learnt by heart polite little speeches about his works. To begin with he regretted his own fireside and the intellectual life of Edinburgh, but by degrees he became reconciled to this social incense.

It pleased Hume that in France, as at home in Scotland, he should be popular also for his personal qualities. The French recognized his real good nature, simplicity and shrewdness. He was quite aware, also, of the contrast between the French and English appreciation of literature. Walpole remarked to him with covert insolence: "You know in England we read their works but seldom or never take notice of authors. We think them sufficiently paid if their books sell, and of course leave them in their colleges and obscurity." To which Hume replied that our enemies would infer from this that England was "fast relapsing into barbarism, ignorance and superstition".

Hertford left Paris in July 1765, and, until the arrival of his successor, the Duke of Richmond in October, Hume was left as *chargé d'affaires*. Brougham, who saw the correspondence of the time, says that Hume proved himself an excellent man of business, wrote good dispatches, obtained useful information, and showed firmness and sagacity. In France he became affectionately known as "Le bon David".

Hume returned to Scotland in 1766, and in the following year was appointed Under Secretary of State for Scottish Affairs. He had real capacity for such a position. He was at all times a man of punctual habits and unwearied industry. Some of the official documents connected with the successive offices he held have fortunately been preserved, and they attract the attention of anyone who examines them not only by the clearness and precision of the language, but even by the neatness of the handwriting.

The historian never married, but took a great interest in the welfare of his relations. In 1769 he was making some enquiries from Edinburgh on behalf of his nephew. In a letter to Sir Gilbert Elliot he writes: "I am very much obliged to you for the pains you have taken to give me an account of your sons' expenses and management at Oxford. I found my brother undetermined, or rather averse, to the project. He thinks his son rather inclines to be dissipated and idle; and believes that a year or two at Oxford would confirm him thoroughly in that habit, without any other advantages than the acquiring of a little better pronunciation; for this reason he seems rather inclined to try him a year in the Law College here before he makes him so much his own master."

It seems a little strange that a man so deservedly popular as Hume should have remained a bachelor. In point of fact, however, he once had very different ideas. When he was still young and poor he proposed to a lady of position and beauty, who promptly rejected him. When he became rich and famous the lady, no longer young and fastidious, sent word by a confidential friend that she had "changed her mind", to which the historian retorted bluntly, "So have I".* By this time he had found contentment in his intellectual pursuits and in the simple pleasures which he enjoyed in the company of his many good friends.

Allan Ramsay painted a portrait of Hume in scarlet and gold lace. On George III suggesting that the dress was too fine, the privileged court painter replied that "he wished posterity to see that one philosopher in His Majesty's reign had a good coat to his back".

In 1770 "Hume the infidel" began building a house in the New Town of Edinburgh. This was the first house in a street leading southwards from St. Andrew Square. When Hume took up residence the street had not yet been named, and a witty young lady, daughter of Lord Ord, chalked on the wall of his house for a frolic the words "St. David Street". The serving lass of the historian, resenting that anyone should make fun of her master, ran to inform him what had happened. "Never

* *Caldwell Papers*, Vol. II, p. 190.

mind, lassie," he said, "many a better man has been made a saint of before." So the name remained, was officially adopted, and still serves as a permanent memorial of the great man in the street in which he spent the latter part of his life.

As a reputed infidel, the historian was regarded by some simple folk as being among the damned, and destined to suffer everlasting torment. But a man so pleasant and genial was not without well-wishers who were anxious to save him from a fate so terrible. One woman who came to see him on such an errand declared that she had received a message from on High. David received her courteously and gravely. "This is an important matter, madam," he said. "We must take it with deliberation— perhaps you had better get a little temporal refreshment before you begin. Lassie, bring this good lady a glass of wine." Then, as she enjoyed the refreshment provided, the philosopher chatted good-humouredly with her and, discovering that her husband was a chandler, declared cunningly that he was greatly in need of candles, and entrusted his guest with a very large order. Delight at this unexpected piece of business drove all other thoughts from the good woman's mind, and, forgetting her important mission, she hurried home at once to tell her husband.

Many other visitors came to the house in St. David's Street to see its hospitable owner, and Professor Huxley remarks that in the following six years it was the centre of the accomplished and refined society which then distinguished Edinburgh.

Hume was on terms of warm friendship with his distant cousin John Home, described as being an admirable companion, tall, very handsome, and with an agreeable address. The two cousins had the same generous nature and the same high spirits, so that when they met the occasion was very apt to become a convivial one. Friendly banter was exchanged about the way their name should be spelt. Another source of amiable difference of opinion was found in their preference for wines being unlike. John regarded claret as the proper drink for a Scot, because of the auld alliance with France, and would not countenance port because the custom of drinking it had arisen from the English alliance with Portugal. David, being more judicious and cosmopolitan, had in his cellar excellent port as well as claret. John voiced his prejudice in this epigrammatic form:

Haughty and fierce the Caledonian stood;
Old was his mutton, and his claret good.
Let him drink port, an English statesman cried;
He drank the poison, and his spirit died.

John Home has some claim to literary eminence as the
author of the tragedy *Douglas,* which was first performed at the
Canongate Theatre in Edinburgh on 14 December 1756. David
Hume provided a dedication, and used his considerable influence
as the leading Scottish man of letters to have the play performed
in London. His efforts on behalf of his kinsman were entirely
successful, and in July 1757, he was able to write to his good
friend the Abbé Le Blanc in Paris in these terms: "In order to
raise it from Obscurity, I wrote to the Author the Dedication,
which had so good an Effect that the Tragedy was brought on in
Covent Garden, and extremely well received by the Public."
The favourable opinion which David had of the work was shared
by others who spoke with authority. Thus on 10 August 1757,
Thomas Gray wrote in a personal letter, "I am greatly struck by
the *Tragedy of Douglas.* The Author seems to me to have
retrieved the true language of the Stage, which has been lost
for these hundred years; and there is one Scene (between Matilda
and the old Peasant), so masterly that it strikes me blind to all
defects."

The motto on the private seal used by David Hume was
"True to the End", and we see how accurately this sentiment
was upheld in the case of his friendships. When in 1776, with
rapidly failing health, he made the journey to Bath to take
the waters there, John came with him, and relieved the tedium
of travel with his pleasant company. So Hume added a codicil
to his will, "I leave to my Friend, Mr. John Home of Kilduff,
ten dozen of my old Claret at his Choice; and one single bottle
of that other Liquor called Port. I also leave to him six dozen
of Port, provided that he attests under his hand, signed John
Hume, that he has himself alone finished that Bottle at two
sittings. By this Concession he will at once terminate the only
two Differences that ever arose between us concerning temporal
matters."

Several friends of Hume left on record their testimony to
his pleasant character. Thus Lord Chief Commissioner Adam
wrote: "His simple, unaffected nature and kindly disposition

exalted him as much as the singular powers of his mind."
Again his friend Adam Smith expressed himself in these terms:
"His temper seemed to be more happily balanced than that
perhaps of any other man I have ever known. Even in the
lowest state of his fortune, his great and necessary frugality
never hindered him from exercising, upon proper occasions,
acts both of charity and generosity. It was a frugality founded,
not upon avarice, but upon the love of independency. The
extreme gentleness of his nature never weakened either the
firmness of his mind or the steadiness of his resolutions. His
constant pleasantry was the genuine effusion of good nature and
good humour, tempered with delicacy and modesty. And that
gaiety of temper, so agreeable in society, but which is so often
accompanied with frivolous and superficial qualities was, in him,
certainly attended with the most severe application, the most
extensive learning, the greatest depth of thought, and a capacity
in every respect the most comprehensive. Upon the whole I have
always considered him, both in his lifetime and since his death,
as approaching as nearly to the idea of a perfectly wise and virtuous man as, perhaps, the nature of human frailty will permit."

These characteristics remained until his death. On 20 August
1776, five days before he died, he wrote to the Comtesse de
Boufflers a letter ending with the words, "I see death approach
gradually, without any anxiety or regret. I salute you, with great
affection and regard, for the last time." Dr. Blake records that
when he was so weakened by his last illness that he could no
longer rise from his bed, he never dropped the smallest expression of impatience; but, when he had occasion to speak to the
people about him, always did it with affection and tenderness,
dying "in such a happy composure of mind that nothing could
exceed it". In the weeks immediately before his death, which
took place on 25 August 1776, he continued to welcome visitors,
and received them with "tranquillity and pleasantry". When
enquiries were made about his health he replied that he was
going as fast as his enemies could wish, and as easily as his
friends could desire. His friend Dr. Cullen wrote: "His senses
and judgment did not fail till the last hour of his life. He
constantly discovered a strong sensibility to the attention and
care of his friends and, amidst great uneasiness and langour,
never betrayed any peevishness or impatience."

Graham, in his *Scottish Men of Letters,* says that during the last illness of the historian his condition was the universal subject of inquiry and interest with high and low in Edinburgh. He was the most popular man in the city, and everyone spoke of him with the anxiety of an intimate friend. When the end came, there was mourning in many homes. On the day of his funeral affection for him caused a large crowd to gather. One man was heard to say, "Ah, he was an atheist", to which another rejoined, "No matter, he was an honest man". Professor T. H. Huxley suggests that some of the people came to see if anything unusual happened. He says that the body was attended by a great concourse of people "who seem to have anticipated for it 'he fate appropriate to the remains of wizards and necromancers". There may have been some truth in this, for in a tract having the title *Curious Particulars respecting David Hume,* published in 1788, it is stated that "After his interment, two trusty persons watched the grave for about eight nights (was this for fear of fanatical outrages?). The watch was set by eight at night, at which time a pistol was fired. Candles in a lanthorn were placed on the grave, where they burned all night." The grave is at a spot selected by Hume himself, in an old burial-ground on the eastern slope of the Carlton Hill.

Some authorities place Hume with Gibbon and Robertson in an English historical triumvirate. Both Gifford and Schlegel rank Hume above Gibbon. And apart from his position as a historian, Smollett called him "one of the best men, and undoubtedly the best writer of the age".

THE HISTORICAL WORKS OF HUME
WITH DATES OF PUBLICATION

1754   *History of Great Britain, containing the Reigns of James I and Charles I,* Vol. I.

1756   *The Revolution,* Vol. II.

1759   *History of England under the house of Tudor,* Vols. III and IV.

1762   *Julius Caesar to the accession of Henry VII,* Vols. V and VI.

Note: It will be observed that as written the sections of Hume's history were not in chronological order. In later editions the parts were arranged in their natural sequence.

ADAM SMITH

from the medallion by Tassie

CHAPTER III

Adam Smith

(1723-1790)

ADAM SMITH was born at Kirkcaldy in Fife on 5 June 1723. His father was sometime Judge Advocate for Scotland, and his mother was Margaret Douglas of Strathhendry, where her family held considerable landed property.

As a boy he attended the Grammar School at Kirkcaldy, where he was popular with the other boys because of his uncommonly friendly and generous disposition, and attracted the notice of the staff because of his passion for books and the extraordinary powers of his memory.

He entered Glasgow University in 1737, and had the good fortune to come under the influence of Professor Francis Hutcheson, a thinker of great original power. Hutcheson was the first professor at Glasgow to give up lecturing in Latin, and to address his students in their own tongue. It was regarded as scandalous that in his lectures he should expound the principles of religious and political liberty. In Smith's first year, in fact, Hutcheson was prosecuted by the local Presbytery for teaching two false and dangerous doctrines: first, that the standard of moral goodness was the promotion of the happiness of others; and second, that we could have a knowledge of good and evil without and prior to a knowledge of God.

Early promise was fulfilled when Smith, after graduating at Glasgow, gained the Snell bursary at Oxford. It was an ordeal to go south of the border. When he went into residence at Balliol he and the few other Scots there found themselves living in painful isolation. The English undergraduates, with the brutal frankness of youth, ridiculed their poverty, their unpolished manners, their tongue and their kirk. And the education offered was poor. Viscount Haldane says that at this time the whole place was weighed down by intellectual listlessness, and by indifference to the rapid movement of the time. Fortunately Smith had a genius that was capable of rising above its environment.

While in residence Adam had to live on very little. His grant was not sufficient to enable him to come home even in vacation time, for the long journey to Scotland would have cost half his funds for a twelve-month. His exile was continuous for six years, and partly because of this long separation from his family he was ill and in poor spirits for most of the time. He studied hard, and in spite of the neglect of his tutors read deeply and widely. Unfortunately he attempted too much, and suffered from lassitude and exhaustion due to overwork. He never fully recovered his health after leaving Oxford.

In his work he made good use of the Balliol library, one of the best possessed by any of the Oxford colleges. He was not encouraged, however, to taste fare other than that officially provided. One day, for example, he was found reading Hume's *Treatise of Human Nature,* which had been presented to him by the author at the suggestion of Professor Hutcheson of his old University. The supposedly evil book was confiscated and he was given a severe reprimand. A great work of modern thought, such as this, was condemned because at the time learning at Oxford was in almost total eclipse.

It had been the hope of Adam's friends and relations that he would take up either an ecclesiastical career, or that he would become a tutor at Oxford. He declined both these openings, however, because he objected to taking holy orders. Then and much later ordination was a condition for the granting of all fellowships at Oxford. So Smith set out for Scotland again, valuing his principles more than worldly success. He appears never to have visited Oxford again, and to have maintained no personal contacts with the university.

Professor Dugald Stewart says that it was well known to Adam's friends that in the early part of his life he was attached for several years to a young lady of great beauty and accomplishment. Circumstances which were never disclosed prevented their union, but neither married anyone else. When the lady was over eighty she still retained evident traces of her former beauty. It was noted, too, that even at that advanced age the powers of her understanding and the gaiety of her temper seemed to have suffered nothing from the hand of time.

Among the earliest friends of Adam Smith were David Hume and Alexander Wedderburn, who became Earl of Rosslyn and

Lord High Chancellor. The friendship with the former was especially happy and intimate. Adam and David were both of singularly contented and amiable disposition. But although the most pleasant of companions, and highly esteemed by their other intimates on that account, their work sometimes showed sharply critical intellectual powers. They had, in fact, minds that were closely attuned; they had the same outlook; and their researches were conducted on parallel lines. Only the death of Hume ended a sympathetic intercourse which remained entirely without shadow and grew constantly more cordial through the years.

In 1751 Adam Smith was chosen as Professor of Logic in the University of Glasgow. One of his students afterwards observed that, "In the professorship of logic Mr. Smith soon saw the necessity of departing widely from the plan that had been followed by his predecessors, and of directing the attention of his pupils to studies of a more interesting and useful nature than the logic and metaphysics of the schools". He introduced, in fact, reforms long overdue, and gained rapidly in reputation. He followed in the footsteps of Professor Hutcheson in doing his utmost to liberalize the system ruling at the university in his day. He even sought to discontinue the opening prayer in his lecture room, but the Faculty would not permit this irreligious omission.

A year afterwards he became professor of Moral Philosophy in the same university. In this higher position also his influence steadily extended. "His lectures were always distinguished by a luminous division of the subject, and by fullness and variety of illustration; and as they were delivered in a plain unaffected manner, they were well calculated to afford pleasure as well as instruction". In a great commercial city like Glasgow the doctrines he expounded naturally aroused great interest, and gave rise to an eager spirit of enquiry. His classroom was crowded with students not only from the immediate locality but from all parts of the country, including the remote Highlands.

He was very sensitive about making sure that he had the interest of even the dullest member of his class. He remarks how, throughout a whole session, one student served him as a guide. "If he leant forward to listen, all was right and I knew I had the ear of my class; but if he leant back in an attitude of listlessness, I felt at once all was wrong and that I must either change the subject or the style of my address."

The professors were poor. Some had obtained their posts by bribing their predecessors to retire by paying them a lump sum, although to do so created a debt which took years to pay off.

In any case so little was received that every item was of consequence, so that Professor Black, for example, "sat at his desk when the students were paying their fees, with a pair of brass scales beside him on which he, with exact nicety weighed the coins, to sift the light guineas from the good". In these circumstances any addition to income was welcome. When the sons of Hieland lairds came to the university members of the professional staff often kept them as boarders, or perhaps it would be more accurate to say that the boarders kept their hosts. There were good and sufficient reasons why Smith and his colleagues should be interested in economics.

Glasgow was very prosperous at this period. A large share had been gained in the colonial trade from which Scotland had been excluded before the Union. These were the days of the great tobacco lords, with great quantities of tobacco being brought to the Clyde, often to be exported later to different parts of Europe. The great mercantile city offered admirable facilities for practical study and investigation to the economist who was willing to work hard. Much attention was being paid to economic questions relating to industrial development, commerce, and agriculture. In general Glasgow was a centre of both intellectual and scientific progress. Adam Smith was always anxious to learn from those about him. He had a kind of second sight, so that he could relate even small things to great economic laws which were beyond the vision of his friends. Nothing escaped his powerful intellect.

The eighteenth century was distinguished by its clubs, "where congenial spirits met once a week and combined chicken-broth with discussions on trade and the fine arts". While Adam Smith was in Glasgow he belonged to the famous Political Economy Club there, which had been founded by a leading merchant, Andrew Cochrane. Through "Cochrane's Club" he was able to keep in constant touch with the most prominent business men of the city.

When Smith succeeded to the Chair of Moral Philosophy he worked out a plan for his lectures in which he divided the science of morals into four parts. The first covered Natural Theology, the second Ethics, the third Justice, and the fourth Economics. His chief interests lay in the second and fourth sections, and to begin with he concentrated upon working out his system of ethics, afterwards to appear as his *Theory of Moral Sentiments*. The first section appears to have been included only because the university authorities expected it, and not from any inclination of his own. For the third section he planned "to give an account of the general principles of law and government, and of the different revolutions they have undergone in the different ages and periods of society", but the project was never carried out.

In 1759 his work on *The Theory of Moral Sentiments* was published from the London bookshop of a fellow Scot named Andrew Millar. The book had both solid and attractive qualities which ensured its success. David Hume sent news of its reception to the author. "The mob of literati are beginning to be loud with praise", he reported. And its publication had remarkable indirect consequences. One of the people who admired it was the Hon. Charles Townshend, stepfather of the Duke of Buccleuch, then a boy. Townshend decided that a man so virtuous, learned, and so well acquainted with human nature was admirably suited to act as governor to his distinguished relative at a later stage in his education. His view did not change, and three years afterwards, when the Duke was old enough to travel, he invited Smith to become his tutor, and even asked the professor to name his own terms, which ᴜe then handsomely exceeded.

The approach was made to Smith in October 1763, when the Duke was about to leave Eton. The terms arranged were for a salary of £300 a year, or twice Smith's income from the Glasgow University, with all travelling expenses while abroad. In addition he was to receive afterwards a pension of £300 a year for life. This was an important provision, for the Scotch professors then received nothing after they had retired unless they made some bargain with their successor. The offer was too tempting to be refused, and the Duke was in the charge of his famous tutor for three years. This relatively short period of service enabled Smith to earn £8,000, for he drew his pension for twenty-four years afterwards. Thus he was not only given the opportunity of obtaining first-hand knowledge of the national economy and way of life of foreign peoples, but upon his return was provided with the private revenue which enabled him to devote ten years of quiet retirement to the patient maturing of his classic work.

The system under which the appointment was made was a well established one. What normally happened was that professors who become tutors did not resign, but were allowed to employ cheap substitutes for the three or four years they were absent. Adam Smith was too high-minded and conscientious to retain his chair and salary in this way. He resigned, therefore, and at the close of his last lecture produced the fees that each member of his class had paid him, neatly wrapped in paper. The first student he called up protested that he had already received more value than he could ever repay, a sentiment that drew applause from the others. His master, however, caught him by the coat, exclaiming, "You must not refuse me this satisfaction. Nay, gentlemen, you shall not!" and thrust the money into the young man's pocket, the rest then coming up reluctantly in turn. Siller is appreciated at its proper value by the Scot, and many of the undergraduates has a stiff struggle to pay their way, so that this little scene had real significance.

The first eighteen months of the tour were spent at Toulouse, followed by some months at Geneva and a year in Paris. Although Adam Smith had a good acquaintance with French literature before he arrived in France his knowledge of the spoken language was very limited. He did not wait to perfect his French, but began his investigations promptly, increasing his great store of illuminating examples of economic principles. This was all the easier because in the early part of their visit he and Buccleuch knew few people and from necessity, therefore, lived in a very retired way.

It was natural for Smith and his pupil to choose Toulouse for a prolonged stay, for it was a favourite resort of British residents in France, and had many intellectual attractions. Here was the seat of an archbishopric, of a university, of a parliament and of a learned academy. Here was a kind of ancient capital, where the nobility of the province had their town houses. Here also was a place entirely French in its characteristics, escaping the cosmopolitan adulteration of Paris as well as the excessive distractions which the latter offered. For the serious student Toulouse was the ideal choice.

Among other introductions Smith had one from Hume to his cousin the Abbé Seignelay Colbert, of an Inverness-shire family, who was then Vicar-General of the diocese of Toulouse. After they had become acquainted the Abbé wrote to Hume thanking him for having introduced Smith and saying, "Mr. Smith is a sublime man. His heart and his mind are equally admirable."

In due course the move to Geneva was made. The celebrated Charles Bonnet, who became one of their firmest Swiss friends, in the course of a letter written to Hume ten years afterwards, asks to be remembered to "the sage of Glasgow", adding: "You perceive I speak of Mr. Smith, whom we shall always recollect with great pleasure."

After Switzerland came Paris. Smith enjoyed Parisian society, and the opportunity of talking with such brilliant men as D'Alembert, Helvétius and Morellet, but it might be said that his heart was in Scotland. In a letter to his publisher Andrew Millar, he wrote: "I am happy here; yet I long to rejoin my old friends. If I once got fairly to your side of the water, I think I should never cross it again." The lengthy exile, though not without its compensations, was a heavy sacrifice for a man of established position.

The return from the Continent was hastened by a terrible event. Buccleuch's brother, Lord Hugh Scott, who had also been placed in the charge of Adam Smith, was murdered in the streets of Paris. The party brought his body back to England.

The three years which Smith had spent in travel abroad gave him great advantages. In addition to a matured cosmopolitan outlook he gained an intimate knowledge of the laws, politics and customs of France. He also made a special study of French agricultural methods. The leading European economists became his friends.

As Morellet came to know Smith well he was able to form a very just estimate of him. "I regard him", he says, "as one of the men who have made the most complete observations and analysis on all questions he treats of." This tribute is of consequence because it shows the respect with which his investigations were regarded by informed contemporaries. The Scot long worked on the same lines of research as his French colleagues, but none of the latter ever claimed that he obtained any of his ideas from them, or that he was in any way under their influence. In point of fact it is not possible to be dogmatic about such a matter, for the original thinkers of any period are subject to the same conditions, and treat of the same things, so that resemblances are inevitable.

The tour was very successful, and Buccleuch said afterwards of his tutor, "In October 1766 we returned to London, after having spent near three years together without the slightest disagreement or coolness; on my part with every advantage that could be expected from the society of such a man. We continued to live in friendship till the hour of his death; and I shall always remain with the impression of having lost a friend whom I loved and respected, not only for his great talents, but for every private virtue." His Grace had, in fact, the heart and understanding to appreciate him, and "could learn nothing ill from a philosopher of the utmost probity and benevolence".

In his university lectures Smith had laid down as early as 1753 the principles of economics which were later to be developed fully in his *Wealth of Nations*. In 1773 he went to London to place the manuscript in the hands of a publisher. He regarded the work as complete apart from the need for a little final revision. So heavy had been his labours, however, that his health was more uncertain than usual, and there was a real danger that he might not live to see his masterpiece through the press. In actual fact his health improved in the capital, and he spent most of the next three years there.

Remarkable consequences arose from Smith's stay in the metropolis. He found that new sources of information were open to him there, and that fresh investigations were desirable. Having the true temperament of the scholar he devoted himself without reservation to new researches of the fullest possible scope. The *Wealth of Nations* as we know it took its final form in these years, for he went through much of it again, chapter by chapter, enriching and enlarging it.

Many of the additions made in the London period relate to colonial or American experience. Smith had, while in Glasgow, the opportunity over many years of discussing the affairs of the American colonies with the merchants and retired planters of that city. Now in London he was able to check his theories, and test the evidence he had already obtained in the north, by obtaining information from fresh quarters. Dr. Franklin of Philadelphia was one of those to whom he turned. Smith was quite open-minded, and even reversed some of his propositions, while hundreds of allusions to colonial conditions and growth were newly incorporated. Although it is evident that he under-estimated the resources of London in advance, he did not fail to make good use of them when he had the chance: he recog-nized the richness of the mine he had struck.

The publication of Adam Smith's *Inquiry into the Nature and Causes of the Wealth of Nations* took place in March 1776. It appeared in two volumes at the price of 36s., and it is believed that the author received a lump sum of £500 for the first edition, which was the same amount that had been paid not long before for Sir James Steuart's *Inquiry into the Principles of Political Economy*.

Sales were good, and the first edition was exhausted in six months. The arrangement suggested by Smith for the second edition was that the profits should be divided equally between author and publisher. This was accepted by Strahan of the publishing firm on behalf of his partner and himself. In a letter to Smith he says that it is a "very fair" proposal, "and therefore very agreeable to Mr. Cadell and me". The publishers had been pleasantly surprised by the success of the first edition. Hume had remarked that the work required too much thought to be as popular as Gibbon's, and Strahan, in the course of a letter to him, states: "What you say of Mr. Gibbon's and Dr. Smith's book is exactly just. The former is the most popular work; but the sale of the latter, though not near so rapid, has been more than I could have expected from a work that requires much thought and reflection (qualities that do not abound among modern readers) to peruse to any purpose."

A. S. Turberville emphasizes the importance of the historical element in Adam Smith's work. He says that he is "most famous as an epoch-making economist, but owing his pre-eminence in

that sphere in no small measure to the extraordinary range of
his general and especially his historical learning".

The publication of the *Wealth of Nations* brought many
congratulations. In April 1776, David Hume, who was already
a sick man and within six months of his death, wrote from
Edinburgh:

I am much pleased with your performance, and the perusal of
it has taken me from a state of anxiety. It was a work of so much
expectation by yourself, by your friends, and by the public, that I
trembled for its appearance; but am now much relieved; not but
that the reading of it necessarily requires so much attention, and
the public is disposed to give so little, that I shall still doubt for
some time of its being at first very popular. But it has depth, and
solidity, and acuteness, and is so much illustrated by curious facts,
that it must at last take the public attention. It is probably much
improved by your last abode in London. If you were here at my
fire-side, I should dispute some of your principles. But these, and
a hundred other points, are fit only to be discussed in conversation.
I hope it will be soon; for I am in a very bad state of health, and
cannot afford a long delay.

In the House of Commons the famous Charles James Fox
commended one of his doctrines, "the way, as my learned friend
Dr. Adam Smith says, for a nation, as well as an individual, to
be rich, is for both to live within their income". How un-
fashionable such a sentiment has become in recent years! Fox
was afterwards on friendly terms with Gibbon, and the latter
made honourable mention of Adam Smith in his Roman history.

The wealth of a people is so intimately connected with all
the details of their civil and political existence that Adam Smith
was inevitably drawn into many curious discussions upon points
somewhat apart from his main theme. In such cases we find
"the same sagacity of observation, the same depth of research,
and the same force of reasoning" as when he is considering
major matters. Some of the facts he gives are extraordinarily
picturesque and illuminating, and attract by the homely and apt
way in which he expresses them. Of fascinating interest, for
example, are the passages dealing with the earnings of labourers
in New York; infant mortality in the Highlands of Scotland;
and the economics of dairy-farming.

In a very interesting and important passage the growth of
the power of the Church is described, followed by an account of

the decline of its influence. "In the ancient state of Europe, before the establishment of arts and manufactures, the wealth of the clergy gave them the same sort of influence over the common people which that of the great barons gave them over their respective vassals, tenants, and retainers. In the great landed estates, which the mistaken piety both of princes and private persons had bestowed upon the church, jurisdictions were established. . . . Over and above the rents of these estates, the clergy possessed in the tithes a very large portion of the rents of all the other estates in every kingdom of Europe. The revenues arising from both those species of rent were, the greater part of them, paid in kind, in corn, wine, cattle, poultry, etc. The quantity exceeded greatly what the clergy could themselves consume; and there were neither arts nor manufacturers for the produce of which they could exchange their surplus. The clergy could derive advantage from this immense surplus in no other way than by employing it, as the great barons employed the like surplus of their revenues, in the most profuse hospitality, and in the most extensive charity. Both the hospitality and the charity of the ancient clergy, accordingly, are said to have been very great. They not only maintained almost the whole poor of every kingdom, but many knights and gentlemen had frequently no other means of subsistence than by travelling about from monastery to monastery, under pretence of devotion, but in reality to enjoy the hospitality of the clergy."

From the tenth to the thirteenth centuries, and for some time afterwards, "the constitution of the church of Rome may be considered as the most formidable combination that ever was formed against the authority and security of civil government, as well as against the liberty, reason, and happiness of mankind, which can flourish only where civil government is able to protect them. In that constitution, the grossest delusions of superstition were supported in such a manner by the private interests of so great a number of people as to put them out of all danger from any assault of human reason."

A change came about with the gradual development of industry and trade. "In the produce of arts, manufactures, and commerce, the clergy, like the great barons, found something for which they could exchange their rude produce, and thereby discovered the means of spending their whole revenues upon their own persons, without giving any considerable share of them to other people. Their charity became gradually less extensive, their hospitality less liberal or less profuse. Their retainers became consequently less numerous, and by degrees dwindled away altogether."

During the fourteenth and fifteenth centuries the temporal power of the church became very much less, and "even her spiritual authority was much weakened when it ceased to be supported by the charity and hospitality of the clergy. The inferior ranks of people no longer looked upon that order as they had done before; as the comforters of their distress, and the relievers of their indigence. On the contrary, they were provoked and disgusted by the vanity, luxury, and expence of the richer clergy, who appeared to spend upon their own pleasures what had always before been regarded as the patrimony of the poor."

Of the ecclesiastics of his own day, also, he has some stern things to say. "In the church of Rome", he observes, "the industry and zeal of the inferior clergy are kept more alive by the powerful motives of self-interest, than perhaps in any established protestant church. The parochial clergy derive, many of them, a very considerable part of their subsistence from the voluntary oblations of the people; a source of revenue which confession gives them many opportunities of improving. The mendicant orders derive their whole subsistence from such oblations. It is with them as with the hussars and light infantry of some armies; no plunder, no pay."

Two cures are suggested for sanctimonius bigotry and gloomy religious intolerance. The first of these remedies is the study of science and philosophy, for "Science is the great antidote to the poison of enthusiasm and superstition". The second is "the frequency and gaiety of public diversions. The state, by encouraging, that is by giving entire liberty to all those who, from their own interest, would attempt without scandal or indecency to amuse and divert the people by painting, poetry, music, dancing; by all sorts of dramatic representations and exhibitions; would easily dissipate, in the greater part of them, that melancholy and gloomy humour, which is almost always the nurse of popular superstition and enthusiasm. Public diversions have always been the objects of dread and hatred to all the fanatical promoters of those popular frenzies. The gaiety and good humours which those diversions inspire, were altogether inconsistent with that temper of mind which was fittest for their purpose, or which they could best work upon. Dramatic representations, besides, frequently exposing their artifices to public ridicule, and sometimes even to public execration, were upon that account, more than all other diversions, the objects of their peculiar abhorrence."

The author of the *Wealth of Nations* is critical about educational systems. "The improvements", he writes, "which in modern times have been made in several branches of philosophy, have not, the greater part of them, been made in universities. Several of those learned societies have chosen to remain, for a long time, the sanctuaries in which exploded systems and obsolete prejudices found shelter and protection, after they had been hunted out of every other corner of the world. In general, the richest and best endowed universities have been slowest in adopting those improvements, and the most averse to permit any considerable change in the established plan of education."

He remarks that although the public schools and universities of Europe were originally intended only for the education of churchmen they gradually drew to themselves the education of the sons of gentlemen and men of fortune. "No better method, it seems, could be fallen upon of spending the long interval between infancy and that period of life at which men begin to apply in good earnest to the real business of the world. The greater part of what is taught in schools and universities, however, does not seem to be the most proper preparation for that business."

Such passages are essential social history, and it has been said of the work as a whole that "it contains many a shrewd and luminous suggestion for the solution of historical and political problems, not a few sagacious and valuable contributions to a science of politics and a philosophy of history".

Although the *Wealth of Nations* has the high degree of originality that only a work of genius can display, it is, of course, possible to trace sources of inspiration. We have seen that during the time Smith spent in Paris he saw much of the economists there. In the first part of his own treatise he follows to some extent the arguments of Turgot, given in the latter's book, *Sur la Formation et la Distribution des Richesses*. But his familiarity with the views and writings of his foreign contemporaries merely added to the wealth of facts upon which he exercised his remarkable native sagacity.

Almost countless English editions of the *Wealth of Nations* followed the original one of 1776, and there were numerous translations. A German translation appeared in 1776-78, a Danish one in 1779-80, and an Italian one in 1780. The first French translation was published in book form in 1781, after appearing in sections in the *Journal de l'Agriculture*. A Spanish translation came out in 1792, though the work had previously been suppressed in Spain by the Inquisition. There was also a Dutch translation in 1796.

In 1787 Adam Smith was elected Lord Rector of the University of Glasgow. He was touched by this notable and kindly tribute from a quarter with which he had had such a long and intimate contact. In his letter of thanks to the Principal he wrote:

"No preferment could have given me so much real satisfaction. No man can owe greater obligations to a society than I do to the University of Glasgow. They educated me; they sent me to Oxford. Soon after my return to Scotland they elected me one of their own members; and afterwards prefered me to another office, to which the abilities and virtues of the never-to-be-forgottten Dr. Hutcheson had given a superior degree of illustration. The period of thirteen years, which I spent as a member of that society, I remember as by far the most useful, and therefore by far the happiest and most honourable period of my life; and now, after three-and-twenty years absence, to be remembered in so very agreeable manner by my old friends and protectors, gives me a heart-felt joy, which I cannot easily express to you."

Literary work of the highest quality is not composed easily. Throughout his life Smith took the utmost pains with all he wrote: the *Wealth of Nations* gives us pleasure because it is literature as well as being a scientific treatise. We can enjoy today as much as when they were written the fresh and vivid descriptions which reveal so intimately the personality and idiosyncrasies of the author. Not long before his death he observed that, after all his practice in writing, he composed as slowly, and with as great difficulty, as at first.

Another way in which he was conscientious was in his determination that only his best work should be preserved. Thus as early as 1773, when, as previously noticed, he was about to leave Scotland for a long absence in London, he wrote in these terms to his most trusted friend, David Hume:

My dear friend,—As I have left the care of all my literary papers to you, I must tell you that, except those which I carry along with me, there are none worth the publication, but a fragment of a great work, which contains a history of the astronomical systems that were successively in fashion down to the time of Des Cartes. Whether that might not be published as a fragment of an intended juvenile work, I leave entirely to your judgment, though I begin to suspect myself that there is more refinement than solidity in some parts of it. This little work you will find in a thin folio paper book in my back-room. All other loose papers which you will find in that desk, or within the glass folding doors of a bureau which stands in my bed-room, together with about eighteen thin paper folio books, which you will likewise find within the same glass folding doors, I desire may be destroyed without any examination. Unless I die very suddenly, I shall take care that the papers I carry with me shall be carefully sent to you.

But the plans of mice and men gang aft agley, and Smith long survived his intended literary executor. His papers were eventually entrusted to Dr. Black and Dr. Hutton, with both of whom he had been intimate for many years. These gentlemen selected a number of essays for publication, which appeared in 1795 under the title of *Essays on Philosophical Subjects*. The contents of the volume show that the author had formed a plan for a connected history of "the liberal sciences and elegant arts", but that it had proved far too extensive to complete before his death. Here, as in his other works, we find that happy combination of full and accurate expression with a gift for apt and picturesque illustration.

Almost from boyhood Smith had the habit of being so preoccupied with his own thoughts that he lost touch with his surroundings. Once he was invited to Dalkeith Palace to meet a politician who was then very much in the public eye. During dinner he fell into a reverie, and began to discourse aloud upon the demerits of his fellow guest in most unguarded terms. When he was recalled to consciousness he was so covered with confusion that he promptly relapsed into reverie again, muttering to himself, "Deil care, deil care, it's all true".

There were two elements in the personality of Adam Smith that deserve special reference. There was first that force of character which enabled him, in spite of poor health, to have such a long and distinguished career and to accomplish so much work of lasting value. In this connection he was a typical hard-headed east-country Scot, "un de ces sages vieux Ecossais", as M. Gounard put it for the "auld alliance". The second element was a certain benignity of disposition that developed in the tranquil years of the latter part of his life. He came to have a calm, detached outlook, evident in such an incident as that in which a young man came to him in the worst days of the American war, bemoaning the ruin of the nation. "Be assured, my young friend," said old Adam, "that there is a great deal of ruin in a nation." It was natural that Edinburgh should be proud of such a citizen when he settled there in the fullness of his fame.

With the passing years Smith's infirmities began to increase, and in 1787, when he was sixty-four years old, he went to London to consult his friend Dr. William Hunter. He was now a national figure, and his friends in the south, famous statesmen as well as scholars, used the occasion of his visit to pay him honour. At one country house he met Addington, Grenville, and William Pitt. As he entered the room the company rose. "Be seated, gentlemen," he said. "No", rejoined Pitt, "we will stand till you are seated first, for we are all your scholars."

And at home in Edinburgh he lived very pleasantly. On Sunday evenings he kept open house, and old and intimate friends came to supper without formality. At about 8 o'clock there was fish and collops and roasted fowls, accompanied by punch and claret, with plenty of good conversation. These agreeable weekly gatherings continued until the end, the last being on the Sunday before he died. He gave his guests a cheerful welcome as usual, but after they had supped and talked it was noticed that he was weary. He was pressed to retire, and as he left the room he paused at the door and said quietly: "My friends, I fear that I must leave this happy meeting, and that I shall never meet you again." His death took place less than a week later, on Saturday, 17 June 1790.

THE HISTORICAL WORK OF ADAM SMITH
WITH DATE OF PUBLICATION

1776 *An Inquiry into the Nature and Causes of the Wealth of Nations.*

START

OLIVER GOLDSMITH

from the portrait by Sir Joshua Reynolds

CHAPTER IV

Oliver Goldsmith
(1728-1774)

It is impressive to consider how wide the achievement of Goldsmith was in the main branches of literature, for he became eminent as novelist, dramatist, poet, essayist and historian. *The Vicar of Wakefield* was the first novel to depict English home life, and is without the coarseness that characterized the work of most earlier novelists. "With that sweet story", says Thackeray, "he has found entry into every castle and every hamlet in Europe." By *She Stoops to Conquer* he achieved the highest dramatic honours, and the play is still frequently performed. Here again we become aware of amazing power and originality, for in contrast to Restoration comedy, so largely concerned with the artificial world of fashion, Goldsmith in the first act of his play puts the action into the hands of the common people. *The Deserted Village* is a work which few poets of a later day have been able to equal. Other immortal verse of "the most beloved of English writers" springs to the mind, like the tender and moving lines:

> When lovely woman stoops to folly,
> And finds too late that men betray,
> What charm can smooth her melancholy,
> What art can wash her guilt away.

Even *Goody Two-Shoes*, one of our best fairy stories, is ascribed to his hand. As a historian, also, his claims are considerable. Washington Irving has said of his works that, "All seem to bespeak his moral as well as his intellectual qualities, and to make us love the man at the same time that we admire the author".

The characteristics of Goldsmith's works are so completely English that it is of interest to consider his descent, for it is commonly assumed that he was Irish in blood because he happened to be born in Ireland. Frank F. Moore, in his *Life of Oliver Goldsmith*, says that, "The Goldsmiths were not, of

course, Irish", and another writer remarks that, "Oliver Goldsmith was of a Protestant and Saxon family settled in Ireland
which, like most other such families, had been in troubled times
harassed and put in fear by the native population". Oliver's
forebears have been traced back to the original member of the
family who came over to Dublin as an officer in the Customs
Service, but no Irish ancestry has been discovered.

Sir James Prior states that the family is English in origin,
and mentions that its coat of arms is similar to that of the
Goldsmiths of Crayford in Kent. The heraldic evidence provided by Sir James leaves little doubt that a close relationship
existed between the two branches. Of the Crayford stock
Francis (1613-55), of St. John's College, Oxford, grandson of Sir
Francis Goldsmith, is known as the translator of Grotius, and
had literary tastes like his kinsman Oliver.

The paternal great-grandfather of Oliver Goldsmith married
Jane, daughter of a Scot named Robert Madden. His grandfather, Robert Goldsmith, gentleman, married Catherine,
daughter of the Very Rev. Dr. Thomas Crofton, D.D., who was
a member of a Lancashire family. His father, the Rev. Charles
Goldsmith, married Ann, daughter of the Rev. Oliver Jones.
It was out of compliment to the Rev. Mr. Jones, who was related
to Oliver Cromwell, that Goldsmith was given the name most
hated by the Irish. He was born in 1728.

Goldsmith obtained the degree of B.A. at Trinity College,
Dublin, in 1749. He was the lowest on the list, but Forster
remarks that it would be pointless to recount the names of
those that appeared above him, as their public merits ended
with their college course, and oblivion has received them.

In view of Goldsmith's Scottish ancestry it is interesting to
note that he took a post-graduate course at the Edinburgh
University. He entered the Medical School there in October
1752. In the winter of that year he wrote to his brother-in-law
Daniel Hodson describing his mode of life: "At night I am in
my lodgings. I have hardly any other society but a Folio book,
a skeleton, my cat, and my meagre landlady. I pay £22 per
annum for Diet, washing and lodging, being the cheapest that
is to be got in Edinburgh." But not all his time was devoted to
study; he had an eye for the lassies, and a little later we find
him asking, "Where will you find a language so prettily become

a pretty mouth as the broad Scotch?" His stay in Scotland was not confined solely to residence in the northern capital, and we find him, for example, visiting the Highlands in the spring of 1753. At this period he speaks with respect of Alexander Monro, the Professor of Anatomy, but later decided to extend his experience by finishing his studies on the Continent. Some relics of his are preserved in the library of the University of Edinburgh, dating back to the days when he was a student there.

From Edinburgh the next place of study chosen by Oliver was the University of Leyden. Then for three years he wandered through Flanders, France, Germany and Italy, availing himself of the hospitality offered to travelling scholars at the different universities. At these establishments he made the customary return by taking part in learned disputations or open academic debates. He is also said to have obtained the degree of M.B. at Louvain or Padua. Apart from any formal recognition, however, his subsequent career shows that he took the utmost advantage of the opportunities open to him of acquiring real culture and learning.

There are certain chemical substances that burn with a light of blinding intensity but are consumed with immense rapidity. A close parallel is to be found in some of the most gifted members of the human race. Among musicians Mozart and Schubert come in this category. Goldsmith, too, died young. In the Reynolds portrait he looks delicate, and his spirit was such a vivid flame that it inevitably burnt itself out quickly. No doubt he overworked, in a magnificent effort to overcome money difficulties, but apart from this he was possessed by a passion to create which was not to be withstood. Until he was nearly thirty his life was crowded with a host of experiences and vicissitudes both at home and abroad that gave him a rich background for his later work. Then followed the brief spell of seventeen years until his death, during which his output was maintained at a level that has hardly been equalled by any other great writer, with an average of at least one major work every twelvemonth.

Goldsmith's nature was such that he had to give the best that was in him. He was not one of those who could debase their talent for the sake of wealth. His attitude in this respect is expressed in his *Inquiry into the Present State of Polite*

Learning in Europe, published at the age of thirty-one when he had not long returned from his sojourns at certain of the famous old universities of the Continent. He writes: "Avarice is the passion of inferior natures; money the pay of the common herd. The author who draws his quill merely to take a purse, no more deserves success than he who presents a pistol."

The versatility of Goldsmith arose partly from his deep human sympathies. He had good feeling as well as good sense. He suffered from hardship and misfortune for many years, yet his outlook remained that of whimsical benevolence. Having been left an orphan at an early age he had full knowledge of adversity, especially as his father, the original of Dr. Primrose in the *Vicar of Wakefield,* was a poor country parson unable to make any adequate provision for his family. So remembering what he himself had had to face we find throughout his life that "His charity seems to have been pushed beyond the limits of prudence, and all who knew him testify to the singular kindliness of his nature". All the salient features of his life show the highest ethical standard as well as great power of intellect. This modest man of genius, so full of goodness and kindness, was also known for his amiability. Some of the finest minds of the time were among his most intimate friends, while the noble, the rich, and the great sought his acquaintance.

How could Goldsmith find the means to move in society, to dress richly, and to return the hospitality that was offered to him? His directly creative works had to be matured slowly, and were the reverse of profitable. Each of them represented considerable self-denial on his part, for to write them meant that he had to withdraw for a comparatively lengthy period from the less vital writing that gave him his living. The main part of his income came from his histories, which made their own contribution to his reputation.

Apart from his limited hours of leisure Goldsmith had to face constant labour to supply his needs. Hume and Robertson were earning both fame and profit by studies of history, and he felt that there was an opportunity for him also in this branch of literature. Material was not lacking, and his skill and taste enabled him to make admirable use of it. Again history not only formed a pleasant variant to his other work, but was a kind of standby task that could be fitted in with other things. To begin with he thought of his historical work chiefly as a source of revenue, but public appreciation was such that he found himself elevated to a height that he had been far too modest to expect in advance. The truth of the matter was that just as lesser men can never write well because of their limited talents, so Goldsmith could not write ill; it was not in him to produce inferior work. He also had certain special advantages as a historian to which reference must now be made.

What kind of history would we expect the author of *The Vicar of Wakefield* to write? This masterpiece is unlike the majority of novels in being short, in contrast to the sprawling, formless novels that were written to order to fill up a certain space. When a publisher stipulated that a novel should occupy three stout volumes, and inspiration was lacking after the first of these, some sorry material was often included in the latter part of a work. The "Vicar", on the other hand is perfect in form, and is all pure gold without any dross. Long dull novels had their counterpart in even longer and duller histories, such as a standard history of Greece that ran to twelve volumes although the author had never visited that country. Goldsmith felt that the essential parts of history could be expressed more briefly than had been the custom, that obscurity could be replaced by clarity, and that freshness of interest could be substituted for ponderous dullness. Such were his aims, and we know that they were well within the scope of his exceptional powers.

Goldsmith wrote in 1761 a *History of the Seven Years' War*, based on some essays he had contributed to the *Literary Magazine* in 1757-58. This history was not printed in full until 1837, when James Prior published it from the original manuscript in the *Miscellaneous Works* of Goldsmith which he edited in that year.

The first historical work by Goldsmith to be published was a *History of Mecklenburgh*. This was commissioned because Mecklenburgh was the country of Queen Charlotte who, at the time it was written, had recently become the bride of George III. The Royal Family was popular, as is shown by the Diary of Fanny Burney, for several years Junior Keeper of the Robes to Queen Charlotte, and hence there was a good deal of public curiosity about Mecklenburgh. This little history was frankly written to meet a need of the moment, and was not published by Goldsmith under his own name. It appeared in 1762, and the author is said to have received £20 for it, an amount which we have to multiply several fold to find the value in money of the present day.

Another piece of minor historical writing undertaken by Goldsmith was his *History of our Own Times,* written in 1763 as a preface to the *General History of the late War* which appeared in that year. These were in the nature of preliminary studies which developed his interest in historical research, and provided him with valuable experience upon which he could draw when he came to write his larger works.

Next came *The History of England in a series of Letters from a Nobleman to his Son,* published in two volumes in June 1764. Here again we find that Goldsmith did not choose to acknowledge the authorship, and the work was issued anonymously. The Mecklenburgh history had been quite successful, but this was much more so. It went through edition after edition, and was attributed to many eminent writers, and first to one peer and then to another. For more than thirty years the authorship remained a mystery, and one of the pirated editions actually bore the name of Lord Lyttleton, himself a historian of repute.

Goldsmith received only £50 for this history, but we have again to remember that because of the difference in the value of money the amount was then much more substantial. The contract too, was made in advance, so that the publisher Newbery accepted some risk. The return to the publisher was a rich one, and the terms obtained by Goldsmith for his later histories reflected this fact.

Having obtained some experience as a historian Goldsmith felt a stronger attraction and interest in this kind of study. He had also acquired a reputation among the publishers for this sort of work, though his name had not yet been revealed to the general public in connection with it. There was, therefore, a keen demand for him to produce more. Prior says that had he devoted himself to the composition of history in extended form we cannot doubt that he would have attained great eminence in it. Mere length, however, is no longer regarded as a virtue. By the standards of today Goldsmith wrote at very appropriate length for his subject. From the beginning there was nothing laboured or pretentious about his historical writings. He continued faithful to his original intention to be brief and natural, and he was aided by that ease of expression which is so difficult to acquire and which is the gift only of the favoured few. Washington Irving says of his earlier writings that "they are characterized by his sound, easy good sense, and the genial graces of his style".

The reception given to the shorter histories served as an encouragement to proceed to something more ambitious in this line. Goldsmith's *Roman History* was a major undertaking. It was commissioned by Thomas Davies the bookseller and his partner in 1767, and was to be completed in two years. The sum to be paid for it was 250 guineas. It was stipulated also that it should appear under Goldsmith's own name. Good progress was made with the work, but in the summer of 1768 Goldsmith decided that residence in town brought too many interruptions, and to give him more leisure for his History of Rome he joined with a Mr. Bott in taking a cottage near Edgeware. The gentleman mentioned had chambers adjoining his own in the Temple. This new abode, although small, had a good garden, and had been built as a country retreat by a man of wealth, who had spared neither trouble nor expense in its decoration.

In his country quarters the historian and his friend found fresh air and retirement. Work was the main objective in seeking this seclusion, but as the distance from town was no more than eight miles they still went up occasionally for dinner there. The hour for dining was made 4 o'clock or earlier, as they found it agreeable to return to their retreat in the cool of the evening. The journey back was not always uneventful. Goldsmith's companion drove a gig, but the skill of his driving depended upon how freely he had indulged in the pleasures of the table. A letter is preserved in which Goldsmith recalls how his friend drove against a wayside post, to the imminent danger of their necks, but sturdily maintained that he was still in the middle of the road.

The admirable arrangement of dividing his time between town and country was kept up for several years. In London he took chambers in the Temple as soon as his circumstances permitted, being first at Garden Court, then in the King's Bench Walk, and finally at Brick Court, where he remained until his death.   In the country, apart from the cottage he shared with Mr. Bott, he lodged for a time at a farm near Hyde, and for another period had rooms with residential facilities at Canonbury House, Islington.   When out of town he wrote with the intense application of one who had found his vocation and was supremely well fitted for it.

In February 1769, Goldsmith visited Oxford in company with Dr. Johnson, and is said to have been granted, *ad eundem*, the degree of M.B.   In May of the same year his *Roman History* appeared, being announced in these terms*:

This day is published in two volumes 8vo., Price 10s. 6d. in boards, or 12s. bound, the Roman History, from the foundation of the City of Rome to the destruction of the Western Empire. Written by Dr. Goldsmith. Printed for S. Baker and C. Leigh in York Street; S. Davies in Russell Street, Covent Garden; and L. Davies in Holborn.

The two volumes contained a thousand pages in all, and covered the history of the State from the earliest time to the fall of the western empire.   The critics pronounced it "seasonable and well-timed", and "an excellent digest of Roman History".   It gained "the applause of the multitude", and was read by "gentlemen and those who are more than cursory readers".   It was popular with students "who could not be induced to peruse more voluminous historians".   It received, in fact, a warm welcome from many different types of reader.

Washington Irving says of the *Roman History* that, "such is its ease, perspicuity, good sense, and the delightful simplicity of its style, that it was well received by the critics, commanded a prompt and extensive sale, and has ever since remained in the hands of the young and old".   F. F. Moore declares that, "the history when it left his hands was a masterpiece.   It fulfilled its object so well that it remained for nearly a century practically without a competitor in the market."

The famous Dr. Johnson, once described as an acute and profound philosopher, broke into a warm eulogy of the author and the work in a conversation with Boswell. "Whether we take Goldsmith", said he, "as a poet, as a comic writer, or as an historian, he stands in the first class."   Boswell: "An historian!

* Public Advertiser, 18 May 1769.

My dear sir, you surely will not rank his compilation of the
Roman History with the works of the other historians of this
age?" Johnson: "Why, who are before him?" Boswell:
"Hume, Robertson, Lord Lyttleton." Johnson: "I have not
read Hume; but doubtless Goldsmith's History is better than
the verbiage of Robertson, or the foppery of Dalrymple."
Boswell: "Will you not admit the superiority of Robertson, in
whose history we find such penetration, such painting?" Johnson: "Sir, you must consider how that penetration and that
painting are employed. It is not history, it is imagination. He
who describes what he never saw, draws from fancy. Robertson paints minds as Sir Joshua paint faces in a history piece;
he imagines an heroic countenance. You must look upon
Robertson's work as a romance, and try it by that standard.
History it is not. Besides, sir, it is the great excellence of a
writer to put into his book as much as his book will hold.
Goldsmith has done this in his history. Now Robertson is
like a man who has packed gold in wool; the wool takes up more
room than the gold. No, sir, I always thought Robertson would
be crushed with his own weight—would be buried under his own
ornaments. Goldsmith tells you shortly all you want to know;
Robertson detains you a great deal too long. No man will read
Robertson's cumbrous detail a second time; but Goldsmith's
plain narrative will please again and again. I would say to
Robertson what an old tutor of a college said to one of his
pupils: 'Read over your compositions, and, whenever you meet
with a passage you think is particularly fine, strike it out!'
Goldsmith's is better than that of Lucius Florus or Eutropius;
and I will venture to say that if you compare him with Vertot
in the same places of the Roman History, you will find that he
excels Vertot. Sir, he has the art of saying everything he has
to say in a pleasing manner."

The comparison of Goldsmith with Robertson made by Dr.
Johnson was shrewd and accurate as well as amusing. Robertson
was apt to be carried away by his own eloquence, and to depart
from the plain narration of past events. We find, for example,
that he makes up speeches sometimes for historical characters,
giving precise words when none were actually recorded, and
expanding what was known of a situation by drawing upon
his imagination. He was thus guilty of dangerous distortion of

facts in a way which Goldsmith, with his better sense of proportion, completely avoided.

In one step Goldsmith had fully established his reputation as a serious historian. Recognition was accorded from the highest quarters. Towards the end of 1768 the Royal Academy of Arts had been instituted. In December 1769, the honorary office bearers were announced*: "Dr. Johnson is appointed Professor of Ancient Literature, and Dr. Goldsmith Professor of History to the Royal Academy." The nominations were made to the Crown by the President, Sir Joshua Reynolds, who also painted Goldsmith's portrait. These first Royal appointments were naturally a mark of high distinction. The honorary offices have been continued to the present day, and give the privilege of a seat at occasional meetings, besides the coveted honour of a place at the annual dinner of the Academicians.

Writing to his brother Maurice in January 1770, Goldsmith says: "The King has lately been pleased to make me professor of Ancient History in a Royal Academy of Painting, which he has just established, but there is no salary annexed, and I took it rather as a compliment to the institution than any benefit to myself. Honours to one in my situation are something like ruffles to one that wants a shirt." In letters such as this the historian purposely discourages relatives who might think that he was acquiring unlimited wealth that he could share with them.

In September 1770, Goldsmith accepted an offer of 50 guineas from Davies to write an Abridgement of his Roman History for the use of schools, to be issued in one volume duodecimo. This task was accomplished in an admirable way, and the resulting book long played a most useful part. As Moore says: "The difficulty of getting a volume of history of any sort that will attract rather than repel a young student was solved by Goldsmith, and since his Histories have been discarded no others that have been written have taken their place."

Immediately the Roman History appeared it became evident that it was likely to prove a gold-mine to the publishers and booksellers. Accordingly within three weeks of its issue the same publishers offered £500 for a History of England in four volumes. The following agreement was drawn up:

* Public Advertiser, 22 December 1769.

Memorandum

Russell Street,
Covent Garden.

It is agreed between Oliver Goldsmith, M.B., on the one hand, and Thomas Davies, bookseller of Russell Street, Covent Garden, on the other, that Oliver Goldsmith shall write for Thomas Davies an History of England, from the birth of the British Empire to the death of George the Second, in four volume octavo, of the size and letter of the Roman History written by Oliver Goldsmith. The said History of England shall be written and compiled in the space of two years from the date hereof. And when the said history is written, and delivered in manuscript, the printer giving his opinion that the quantity above mentioned is completed, that then Oliver Goldsmith shall be paid by Thomas Davies the sum of five hundred pounds sterling, for having written and compiled the same. It is agreed also that Oliver Goldsmith shall print his name to the said work.

In witness thereof we have set our names, this 13th of June, 1769.

Oliver Goldsmith
Thomas Davies.

It is to be noticed how faithfully Goldsmith fulfilled his contracts. His *History of England* punctually appeared in August 1771,* or two years and two months from the signing of the agreement. It had of course been *written* in less time than is shown by the date of publication, and no doubt within the two years stipulated. His appearances in fashionable and artistic society had always this foundation of hard work, upon which his greatness was built.

It will be evident that Goldsmith, in considering the history of England, was to some extent re-treading in his own footsteps. Many passages were in fact transcribed verbatim from his "Letters of a Nobleman to his Son", and others were varied merely by the introduction of a few words. The labour of research was lessened in this way, and the critics failed to notice the borrowing. It might have been inconvenient if any discovery had been made, for as the earlier work was anonymous it would have appeared that the historian was using the material of a stranger, though in reality it was his own.

In writing his *History of England,* Goldsmith had the merit of having read widely on the subject. Among the authorities he consulted were Carte, Rafin, Hume and Smollet. He sought

* *Public Advertiser,* 6 August 1771.

to give a succinct and pleasing abstract of our known annals. It was generally agreed that English history had never before been "so usefully, so elegantly and so agreeably epitomized".

If Goldsmith had been less generous in money matters the earnings from his histories and other works, although very inadequate according to modern standards, might have been sufficient for his needs. His nature was, however, too free and open for this to be possible. Thus both from inclination and necessity he soon began the writing of another historical work.

It appears that Goldsmith began writing his *History of Greece* in 1772. By the middle of the following year one volume had been completed, and he received a payment from the publishers through their agent William Griffin. His receipt was in this form:

June 22nd. 1773.

Received two hundred and fifty pounds for writing and compiling the History of Greece from Mr. William Griffin, for which I promise further assignment on demand.

Oliver Goldsmith.

In the introduction he says that: "The fabulous age of Greece must have no place in history; it is now too late to separate those parts which may have a real foundation in nature from those which we owe to folly and the imagination. There are no traces left to guide us in that intricate pursuit; the dews of the morning are past, and it is vain to attempt continuing the chase in meridian splendour." This admirable caution on the part of the historian was necessary, for much of what had previously passed for Greek history had been in the form of fables of a people wishing to claim kindred qualities with the divinities they worshipped. As Goldsmith puts it: "Man, plain historical man, seems to have no share in the picture."

It is recorded that, while at his desk composing the latter part of the work, Goldsmith received a call at his rooms in the Temple from his fellow-historian Gibbon, who was then a comparatively young man. Some points of mutual interest regarding the history were discussed between them.

A clear indication of the quality of a man can often be gained from his choice of friends. In his latter years Goldsmith was beloved by many people, and could select his intimates where he would. Some of his social contacts were with men in high positions like Lord Clare, whom he visited at Bath and who is commemorated in the admirable *Haunch of Venison*. But his closest friendship was with the Hornecks, a Devonshire family of good standing. There was a widowed mother, a son who was in the Guards, an elder daughter Catherine whom Goldsmith called "Little Comedy", and a younger one Mary whom he called "the Jessamy Bride". Mutual regard and sympathetic understanding grew up between Goldsmith and these cultured and kindly people, and he acted as escort when Mrs. Horneck and her daughters visited the Continent in 1770.

Unfortunately innocence and virtue often attract the attention of malice and jealousy, and in 1773 Goldsmith's old enemy Kenrick wrote a letter to a London paper in which he alluded to Oliver's passion for "the lovely H—k." The identity of the writer of the letter was hidden under a pen-name, but Goldsmith went to the publisher, a man named Evans, and chastised him with a cane. Legal proceedings were threatened by the editor, and Goldsmith found himself in a difficult position, because he did not wish publicity regarding the incident to bring distress to the Hornecks. Out of chivalry, therefore, he agreed to pay £50 to a charity—a Welsh one because of Evans. The amount, considering the change in value of money, would have been a substantial one for a rich man, and Goldsmith was poor. He relieved his feeling by writing a dignified protest to the papers about the undoubted "licentiousness" of the press.

Although Goldsmith was most punctilious in fulfilling his engagements with publishers, and always finished work by the contract date, he placed himself at a disadvantage by accepting payments in advance. By anticipating his income in this way he became increasingly in debt to the publishers, who in consequence were probably able to drive hard bargains with him. In his latter years, too, he suffered much from illness, although he continued to work at high pressure. In spite of his difficulties he faced the world with gallant good humour, just as he accepted in good part the very imperfect appreciation of his qualities shown by his contemporaries, and even the crude banter of companions like Dr. Johnson, whose minds were of too coarse a fibre to realize how sensitive his mind was, and how greatly his quality exceeded theirs. But ill-health and growing financial embarrassment had their effect even upon him, and we know that, tragically, he died unhappy. It was at the age of forty-five that the illness began from which Goldsmith never recovered. He was attended by Dr. Fordyce and Dr. Turton. The latter, thinking that his pulse was more irregular than it should be, asked if his mind was at ease, to which Goldsmith replied, "It is not!"

The death of Goldsmith caused great distress to his friends. It is said that Burke burst into tears at the news, and that Reynolds, his most beloved friend, gave up painting for the day. The last illness had begun shortly after Goldsmith had completed his *History of Greece*, and his life-blood may be said to have ebbed with the effort he gave to that work. He died on 4 April 1774, and the history was published two months later, on 15 June.

Goldsmith himself was unmarried. His nephew Henry, who was in the army, left two sons, Commander Charles Goldsmith, R.N., and Lieut. Hugh Colvill Goldsmith, R.N. With these two latter this branch of the Goldsmith family came to an end.

Whatever reputation a man may enjoy during his lifetime the ultimate test must be when his work is submitted to the awesome tribunal of posterity. Humbug and pretence are then swept away, and truth stands revealed. Under this most searching of examinations Goldsmith's histories have proved their worth. It is instructive in this connection to observe the regularity with which the public demanded fresh editions of his histories for a century or more after his death.

In considering the status of Goldsmith as a historian it is essential to have due regard to the fact that he was a pioneer in this field. He was strictly the contemporary of Hume and Adam Smith, both of whom survived him. Like them he had the advantage of long university training and of extensive travel on the Continent. Hume, Adam Smith and Robertson were all Scots, so that Goldsmith takes senior place so far as English historians in the modern sense are concerned. Gibbon was his junior, although here again there was a striking similarity of education and experience.

In breaking new ground Goldsmith was not in the convenient position of being able to follow others. He consulted some of the works of French authorities, who had begun to write history slightly earlier than we did, but in the main others following him. The years that he spent on the Continent at the outset of his career were of service to him in his research because his command of languages, especially Latin and French, permitted him to turn to works in their original tongues which were not available in English.

There is strong evidence that another consequence of Goldsmith's sojourn in foreign parts was that he gained a cosmopolitan point of view, and became, in his own phrase, "a Citizen of the World". It was perhaps an outcome of this that his histories, besides being famous at home for generations, were highly esteemed for a long period in Europe, America and elsewhere. The list of the principal editions of his historical works is impressive.

Of the *Roman History* which, as we have seen, was originally published in 1769, there were many English editions. An Italian edition was printed in Naples in 1810 and another in Milan in 1815. The illustrated French edition of 1805 was followed by one issued in Paris in 1816. A Dutch edition was published in Rotterdam in 1826. The first American edition appeared in Baltimore in 1818, with others in New York in 1820 and Ithaca in 1840.

Of the *History of England* also, very numerous editions followed the original one of 1771. In 1819 the 11th edition, with a continuation by G. Coote, was published in London. In 1831 there was a revised edition in three volumes, with a continuation to the death of George IV. In 1837 came a new four-volume edition, with notes and a continuation to 1836 by E. Bellchambers. In 1840 R. Simpson brought out an Edinburgh edition. In 1858 the 46th edition appeared. In 1862 there was a new edition "re-edited and continued to the death of Prince Albert by a member of the University of London". In 1874, more than a hundred years after its first publication, there was yet another edition, which bore the title, *English History for Woolwich and Army Candidates. From Goldsmith's text.*

An abridgement of Goldsmith's *History of England* enjoyed a popularity almost as great as the full-scale work. An edition of this published in 1793 was "continued by an eminent writer to the present time". A Winchester edition of 1812 was "continued by an eminent historian to the Peace of Amiens, A.D.

1802". A Derby edition of 1819 was "continued by an able writer, and brought down to the present time by an attentive observer of public events". In 1827 E. Code continued the work "to the death of the Duke of York". J. Bigland re-edited it in 1828, and there was another edition in 1831.

Translations of the *English History* appeared fairly frequently. There was a French edition of 1788 and another in 1837. A Spanish edition appeared in Madrid in 1853. A German edition was published in Leipzig in 1862. The Abridgement, continued to 1802, was translated into Bengali by F. Carey, and published at Serampore in 1820.

The *Grecian History* from its appearance in 1774, had a very similar record of success and appreciation to that of the earlier Goldsmith histories. It would be tedious to recount all the editions published, of which there were dozens, but some curious features may be noticed. For example in 1801 an abridged edition was issued, but a generation later we have—"Pinnock's improved editions of Dr. Goldsmith's *History of Greece*, abridged. Ninth edition, augmented by W. C. Taylor, London 1831." In other words the vitality of the work was such that it could be contracted or expanded at will, like a concertina. And editors followed each other in an endless procession, relying on each other, so that we find, for instance—"Whittaker's improved edition of Pinnock's Goldsmith's *History of Greece*, very considerably enlarged. 1857". Thus "Big fleas have little fleas upon their backs to bite 'em, and little fleas have littler fleas, and so on *ad infinitum.*"

A popular work was J. G. Gorton's *Five Hundred Questions deduced from Goldsmith's History of Greece*, published in 1816. There was a fresh edition of this in 1818, while in about 1830 a similar book was based on Goldsmith's *History of Rome.*

The *Grecian History* was brought out in an American edition at Hartford, U.S.A., in 1828, with a further edition there two years later. The work was translated into Greek in 1806, and published in two volumes. The following year an Italian edition was called for. In the middle of the nineteenth century a new Italian edition was required—*Compendio della Storia Greca del dott. Goldsmith, tradotto da F. F. Villardi, Venezia, 1850.*

THE HISTORICAL WORKS OF GOLDSMITH
WITH DATES OF PUBLICATION

1761   *History of the Seven Years' War.*

1762   *History of Mecklenburgh.*

1763   *History of our own Times.*

1764   *The History of England in a series of Letters from a Nobleman to his Son.*

1769   *The Roman History, from the foundation of the city of Rome to the destruction of the Western Empire.*

1771   *The History of England.*

1774   *The History of Greece . . . (published posthumously).*

E

CHAPTER V

Edward Gibbon

(1737-1794)

IN a familiar passage in his Autobiography, the historian claims distinguished ancestry. The details were taken from a book which had fallen into his hands by accident, and in fact none of his pretensions had any proper foundation of truth. Elsewhere in his memoirs he admits quite openly the complete ignorance of the family about its origins. In the latter place Gibbon says: "Beyond these (his father and grandfather) I found neither tradition nor memorial; and as our genealogy was never a topic of family conversation, it might seem probable that my grandfather, the Director of the South Sea Company, was himself a son of earth, who had raised himself from the Work-house or the Cottage."

The Gibbon grandfather rose to affluence in the space of a very few years by acting as an army contractor. It was then immensely lucrative to supply weevil-infested biscuits and shoddy uniforms to men who had no possible means of redress. Even more profitable was the device of charging, with the connivance of high officials who had been corrupted, for goods that had never been supplied. Long afterwards Nelson found the same kind of abuse in the Navy, and we have this record* of the action he took while in command of the West Indies station in 1787:

During his stay upon this station he had ample opportunity of observing the scandalous practices of the contractors, prize-agents, and other persons in the West Indies connected with the naval service. When he was first left with the command, and bills were brought to him to sign for money which was owing for goods purchased for the Navy, he required the original voucher, that he might examine whether those goods had been really purchased at the market price: but to produce vouchers would not have been convenient, and therefore, was not the custom. Upon this Nelson wrote to Sir Charles Middleton, then comptroller of the Navy, representing the abuses which were likely to be practised in this manner.

*Life of Nelson by Robert Southey, LL.D., 1830 edition, pp. 47-48.

EDWARD GIBBON
from the painting by Sir Joshua Reynolds

The answer which he received seemed to imply that the old forms were thought sufficient. Soon afterwards two Antigua merchants informed him that they were privy to great frauds, which had been committed upon government in various departments: at Antigua, to the amount of nearly £500,000; at Lucie, £300,000; at Barbadoes; at Jamaica, upwards of a million. The informers were both shrewd, sensible men of business; they did not affect to be actuated by a sense of justice, but required a percentage upon so much as government should actually recover through their means. Nelson examined the books and papers which they produced, and was convinced that government had been most infamously plundered. These accounts he sent home to the different departments which had been defrauded; but the peculators were too powerful; and they succeeded not merely in impeding inquiry, but even in raising prejudices against Nelson at the board of admiralty, which it was many years before he could subdue. Owing, probably, to these prejudices, and the influence of the peculators, he was treated, on his return to England, in a manner which had nearly driven him from the service.

Gibbon's grandfather founded the family fortunes in this kind of way, and proceeded to even greater lengths. He became a director of the South Sea Company, and on the breaking of the bubble his property was largely confiscated under the Act of Pains and Penalties. Out of assets valued at £106,543 5s. 6d., he was allowed to keep only £10,000. But one so experienced in nefarious practices was not to be kept tethered, and even after his serious South Sea set-back he soon began to accumulate wealth again. At his death in 1736 he was the owner of large landed property.

The father of the historian was of a very different type. He was trained to spend and not to earn: he was the first gentleman of the family. At the age of nine, in 1716, he was sent to school at Westminster, for the prosperous army contractor had social ambitions, but was removed four years later, in "the fatal year twenty" when the South Sea bubble burst. He was later at Emmanuel College, Cambridge, but did not succeed in taking a degree. He appears to have been weak and foolish in character, dissipating a substantial part of his patrimony in speculation and fashionable gambling. In middle-life his losses made it impossible for him to continue to live in town, and he retired to Buriton Manor House, a lesser country residence in Hampshire, which had been entailed upon him.

Edward Gibbon the historian was born in 1737, and was brought up at Buriton. At the age of fifteen he entered Magdalen College, Oxford, which in his day had sunk deep into intellectual sloth. "The fellows of my time", he says, "were decent easy men who supinely enjoyed the gifts of the founder; their days were filled by a series of uniform employments; the chapel and the hall, the coffee-house and the common room, till they retired, weary and well satisfied, to a long slumber. From the toil of reading, or thinking, or writing, they had absolved their conscience; and the first shoots of learning and ingenuity withered in the ground, without yielding any fruits to the owners or the public. . . . Their conversation stagnated in a round of college business, Tory politics, personal anecdotes, and private scandal; their dull and deep potations excused the brisk intemperance of youth." The university was at this period plunged in port and prejudice.

After little more than a year at Oxford the future historian, developing an early but immature interest in theological matters, was received into the Roman Catholic Church. In consequence he was obliged to leave the university and was sent abroad. The months he spent at Oxford he describes as "the most idle and unprofitable of my whole life". Partly with the aim of correcting his religious views, his father placed him in the household of a Calvinist clergyman of Lausanne, and on Christmas Day 1754, he did in fact return to the Protestant Church. The five years he spent on the Continent at this time were of lasting advantage to him and gave him a broader outlook.

In the latter part of his stay at Lausanne, at the age of twenty, Gibbon fell in love with Suzanne Curchod, the daughter of a Swiss pastor. The girl had beauty, wit, charm and intelligence. Of good education, she took the lead in the youthful society of the district. It is not surprising that Gibbon was attracted in spite of his cold and shallow nature. How far his feelings were really involved it is hard to gauge, but he pressed his suit and the lady became passionately attached to him. For a man of character the way was open to great happiness, but at this decisive testing-time the historian revealed the miserable stuff of his make-up.

Gibbon applied to his father for permission to marry Suzanne, but was refused. The plans of the father were very different, for though he himself had just married as his second wife a woman of some fortune, he was in serious financial difficulties, and wished his son also to marry an heiress. So the request from the young man caused him alarm and anxiety. Gibbon, who had become betrothed to Mademoiselle Curchod, was summoned home on the eve of his twenty-first birthday. On his return the money matters of his parent were revealed to him. As soon as he was of age he obliged his father by cutting off the entail of Buriton Manor, in return for the promise of an annuity of £300. This enabled the father to borrow £10,000 on the property, and he became in a good humour with his son, although not, of course, with any thought of allowing him to marry some obscure foreign girl. He was very willing, on the other hand, for his son to cut a figure in society, indulge in fashionable dissipation, or amuse himself in any conventional way.

After the spineless capitulation to his father in signing away his inheritance, Gibbon had at least acquired independence through coming of age and having the promise of £300 a year, however doubtful the security of the latter might be. But being cold-blooded or poor-spirited or both, he wrote to poor Suzanne to break off the engagement. Being a gentleman of the second generation, with all the thick-skinned arrogance of the English milord, he probably felt superior to the young gentlewoman who had entrusted her heart to his keeping.

When Gibbon cancelled the engagement from England, Suzanne was heartbroken, and wrote asking him not to give her up. Low says: "This letter is a passionate outpouring of feeling, unstudied and incoherent in places, and apparently broken off and resumed more than once." There are passages in it such as "Vous êtes le seul homme pour qui j'aye versé des larmes, le seul dont la perte m'ait arraché des sanglots et que tant d'autres me paroissent insipides comparés avec le seul . . .". But Gibbon did not mind what suffering he caused, although for a while he sometimes became sentimental over his wine when dining out with the petty squires round Buriton. Suzanne, too, was young enough for the wound to heal gradually, and the beautiful and accomplished girl lived to become the wife of the celebrated French statesman, M. Necker, and the mother of the gifted and illustrious Madame de Staël.

Gibbon's excuse for his conduct was that he had to rely upon his father's support, and therefore had to submit meekly to his will. As a gentleman he could not, of course, earn his own living. How contemptible are these shifts to avoid some form of industry, the essential and universal condition of existence. It is a denial of life to withdraw from the heat of the conflict. The historian's grandfather may have been an unscrupulous scoundrel, but he did at least live vividly. Nature takes its revenge upon those who fail to fulfil her conditions. Gibbon was denied the happiness of family life or the hope of posterity. Even his historical writing was arid and barren, in so far as the *Decline and Fall* was infinitely more remote from real life than, for example, the *Wealth of Nations*.

Apart from the romance with Mademoiselle Curchod, the time Gibbon spent at Lausanne had not been specially enjoyable. Madame Pavilliard, the wife of the clergyman with whom he lodged, abused and half-starved him. In a suppressed passage of his memoirs he says: "I can now speak of her without resentment, but in sober truth she was ugly, dirty, proud, ill-tempered, and covetous." What would he have said if he *had* been resentful? So in some ways the return to England was a welcome change. Very shortly he was given the opportunity of testing the gaieties of London, and noted rather bitterly afterwards that: "The pleasures of a town-life are within the reach of every man who is regardless of his health, his money, and his company. By the contagion of example I was sometimes seduced. . . . My father's taste had always preferred the highest and the lowest company; and, after twelve years' retirement, he was no longer in the memory of the great with whom he had associated. I found myself a stranger in the midst of a vast and unknown city." This naively self-revealing statement shows that he had still not learnt how to make good use of his time, and suggests that he was occupying himself in the capital much as he had done on the Continent, where his record had not been altogether creditable and where he had had some gambling debts which his family had declined to pay. After nine months in London he returned to Buriton, noting that "on the approach of spring, I withdrew without reluctance from the noisy and extensive scene of crowds without company, and dissipation without pleasure".

In June 1759, during the war with France, Gibbon received a commission as Captain in the South Hampshire Militia, or what would now be called the Territorial Forces. He expected that the duties would be of a nominal nature, but events went badly on the Continent and in the following year the Government received intelligence that the French ports were busy with preparations for the invasion of England. There was thus an immediate threat to the southern counties, and in June 1760 the historian's Battalion was embodied.

Training was undertaken first at Winchester and then at Blandford. Gibbon recorded that, "I hardly took a book in my hand the whole time there. The first two months at Blandford I might have done something, but the novelty of the thing, our field-days, our dinners abroad, and the drinking and late hours we got into, prevented any serious reflection." The officers were mostly fox-hunting, claret-drinking squires, and to begin with the men were a "rabble of rustics", although military discipline and smartness was gradually acquired in fair measure. The historian took his soldiering seriously, but in his Autobiography he notes that, "Amid the perpetual hurry of an inn, a barrack, or a guard-room, all literary ideas were banished from my mind".

Field exercises and the general open-air life improved Gibbon's health, and a certain natural gluttony did less harm at this time than at any other period of his life. But hard drinking was the rule, especially when the war began to take a favourable turn. He notes how merry the Mess was one day after the Colonel, Sir Thomas Worsley, a jovial but choleric man, had returned from undergoing a cure for his gout. Long after tattoo roll-call "Sir Thomas kept still assuring us after every fresh bottle how infinitely sober he had grown". And next day is the rueful comment: "I felt the usual consequences of Sir Thomas's company, and lost a morning because I had lost the day before."

When the regiment entertained there were more unseemly orgies. For a time the corps was stationed near Southampton, and Colonel John Wilkes, who commanded the Bucks Militia in camp close at hand, would sometimes come over and spend the night. On such occasions Wilkes brought with him a baboon dressed up as Satan, or, as some of the men suggested with horror, Satan dressed up as a baboon. Gibbon, who had low tastes, liked Wilkes—"I scarcely ever met with a better companion; he has inexhaustible wit and humour and a great deal of knowledge." He was queer company for the younger man, who writes: "This proved a very debauched day. We drank a good deal both after dinner and supper; and when at least Wilkes had retired, Sir Thomas and some others, of whom I was not one, broke into his room and made him drink a bottle of claret in bed."

Gibbon served for eleven years. In 1763 he was promoted Major, and in 1766 Lieut.-Colonel Commanding in succession to old Sir Thomas. He retired in 1770. Himself a vain man, he came to take great pride in his regiment, and maintained a good state of efficiency. Only two and a half years of the total period were spent under arms and away from home, "condemned", as Gibbon puts it, "to a wandering life of military servitude", but, he observes, "In this peaceful service, I imbibed the rudiments of the language and science of tactics", and "The discipline and evolutions of a modern battalion gave me a clearer notion of the phalanx and the legion". As a comfort-loving man he would not deliberately have chosen this form of experience, but having gained it, as it were accidentally, he was able to turn it to some account.

The Militia period was quite unproductive except for the appearance of a slight work entitled, *Essai sur L'Étude de la Littérature*, published at London in 1761. In later life the author says of his choice of the French language that his "true motive was doubtless the ambition of a new and singular fame, an Englishman claiming a place among the writers of France". In any case the essay was still-born, so that it would have brought neither hurt nor benefit to anyone if it had been written in Chinese. It does, however, represent the first stirrings of literary endeavour.

After his service in the Militia, disembodied in 1763 at the close of the war, freedom was attractive, and Gibbon felt a strong urge to travel again, causing him to make a lengthy continental tour. He lived for a time in Paris, then in Lausanne again, and finally made his way to Italy. He remarks that, "It was at Rome, on the 15th of October, 1764, as I sat musing amidst the ruins of the Capitol, that the idea of writing the decline and fall of the city first started to my mind". He continues: "But my plan was circumscribed to the decay of the city rather than of the empire; and though my reading and reflections began to point towards that object, some years elapsed, and several avocations intervened, before I was seriously engaged in the execution of that laborious work." It is instructive to notice the growth of the project under his hand. No doubt the development of a great work far beyond what was originally conceived is of fairly frequent occurrence. As in a novel or poem, a history takes on a character of its own, and not even the author can foresee just what the outcome of his years of labour will be.

Through living so long abroad Gibbon was very much at ease with French, and wrote the first section of an account of the Rise of the Swiss Republic in that language. He sent the manuscript to David Hume for criticism, and the latter wrote to him in these terms:

London, 24th of Oct., 1767.

Sir,

It is but a few days ago since Mr. Deyverdun put your manuscript into my hands, and I have perused it with great pleasure and satisfaction. I have only one objection, derived from the language in which it is written. Why do you compose in French, and carry faggots into the wood, as Horace says with regard to Romans who wrote in Greek? I grant that you have a like motive to those Romans, and adopt a language much more generally diffused than your native tongue: but have you not remarked the fate of those two ancient languages in following ages? The Latin, though then less celebrated, and confined to more narrow limits, has in some measure outlived the Greek, and is now more generally understood by men of letters. Let the French, therefore, triumph in the present diffusion of their tongue. Our solid and increasing establishments in America, where we need less dread the inundation of Barbarians, promise a superior stability and duration to the English language.

Your use of the French tongue has also led you into a style more poetical and figurative, and more highly coloured, than our language seems to admit of in historical productions: for such is the practice of French writers, particularly the more recent ones, who illuminate their pictures more than custom will permit us. On the whole your History, in my opinion, is written with spirit and judgment; and I exhort you very earnestly to continue it. The objections that occurred to me on reading it were so frivolous that I shall not trouble you with them, and should, I believe, have a difficulty to recollect them. I am, with great esteem, Sir, your most obedient, and most humble Servant,

David Hume.

It is interesting to observe Hume's prophetic note about the future influence of America, and his just appreciation of the growing importance of the English language. Gibbon, who had given two years to the work, found the condemnation painful, but wrote: "I delivered my imperfect sheets to the flames, and for ever renounced a design in which some expense, much labour, and more time, had been so vainly consumed." Perhaps he really did intend to burn the manuscript, but he was always very much the *poseur*, and in fact neglected to do so, the essay being later in the possession of his friend Lord Sheffield. The historian adds: "My ancient habits encouraged me to write in French for the continent of Europe; but I was conscious myself that my style, above prose and below poetry, degenerated into a verbose and turgid declamation. Perhaps I may impute the failure to the injudicious choice of a foreign language."

The time spent by Gibbon on what he regarded as a fruitless venture, no doubt brought him considerable indirect benefits. He gained experience in research and practice in writing. Without some such period of apprenticeship one cannot conceive that it would have been possible for him to embark upon the composition of a major historical work like the *Decline and Fall* with any real hope of achieving success. He was impatient for fame before he had taken the full measure of the labour before him.

Another reason why Gibbon abandoned the Swiss project was because he found that the materials of this history were inaccessible to him, being fast locked in the obscurity of what he termed "an old barbarous German dialect". It is regrettably noticeable how readily the man with some classical training condemns more modern tongues as barbarous.

Again, in contrast with the inspiring Swiss theme, showing a poor, warlike but virtuous Republic emerging into glory and freedom, he considered writing a *History of the Republic of Florence* under the Medicis, showing a Commonwealth that was soft, opulent and corrupt, which by degrees descended from the abuse to the loss of her liberty. It seemed to Gibbon, with his rather cynical outlook, that perhaps both lessons were equally instructive.

For a time Gibbon was in Parliament, but never spoke in debate. His seat was the pocket borough of Liskeard, of which the "owner" was his kinsman, Edward Eliot. His admitted aim in entering politics was to secure one of the well-paid sinecures then available through political patronage (a system not un-known in these later days of nationalized industries), and this object he achieved. He had to wait for some time, however, for although elected to the Commons in 1774, it was not until 1779 that he became a Lord Commissioner of Trade and Planta-tions, with a salary of £750 a year, worth a great deal more then than it would be now. The whole affair was another reflection of his cold, selfish and calculating nature, and he was quite without shame in writing in these terms to his friend Dey-verdun: "You have not forgotten that I went into Parliament without patriotism and without ambition, and that all my views tended to the convenient and respectable [sic] place of a lord of trade. That situation I at length obtained."

His reward came for voting as he was told, and the income was no doubt very useful to him in view of the straitened circum-stances of his spendthrift father and his own expensive tastes. This feature of his career is very like a corresponding one in that of Macaulay, but the latter obtained a richer prize because his acceptability as a speaker made him more valuable to his party. The office Gibbon held was abolished in 1782, and it is significant that in the very next year he resigned from Parliament and went to live permanently with Deyverdun at Lausanne. It is clear that throughout the episode any idea of public service was altogether absent from his mind.

The first quarto volume of the *Decline and Fall* appeared in 1776, following by the second and third volumes in 1781, and the remaining three volumes in 1788. From the commencement of publication the work gained a great reputation, and Gibbon was elected Professor of History to the Royal Academy in succes-sion to Goldsmith. The reasons for this favourable reception were complex in character. There was the morbid preoccupa-tion of the British educational system with the teaching of the classics: a bondage from which our schools and universities are by no means fully emancipated today. There was the fact that no English author had dealt with the subject so exhaustively before, so that the work to some extent filled a gap. Again Bury suggests that success was due to Gibbon's scorn for the Church, which "spiced the book" and excited interest.

It is desirable to estimate the resources available to Gibbon. He may be regarded as a product of French scholarship, for in the libraries of Lausanne it was French authorities in the main that could be consulted. Fréret and de la Bletterie were early favourites with him. Of Tillemont's *Histoire des Empereurs* he writes: "It is much better to read this part of the Augustan history in so learned and exact a compilation than in the originals." Incidentally Bury remarks that, "From the historical, though not from the literary point of view, Gibbon deserted by Tillemont distinctly declines".

While his main debt was due to his French predecessor Tillemont, he made much use of Procopius, the Byzantine historian, whose writings he accepted with a wholesale credulity that was far from being warranted. For the history of Mohammed he, in common with contemporaries, took without question the dubious material to be found in the romance of Al Wakidi. His knowledge of the classical tongues was probably negligible, but this would be no great handicap, as the authorities he needed to consult were practically all available in French. His sources, too, were all conveniently available in printed form; he faced no such colossal task as Froude, who spoke of having consulted over 100,000 papers in manuscript, at home and abroad.

There was impressive bulk in Gibbon's "encyclopaedic" history, and appreciation has been expressed for his power of moulding into a narrative a bewildering multitude of details. Unfortunately for his reputation, critical examination since his day has shown that for the sake of coherence, however imperfectly achieved, he manipulated his material and selected the facts that suited him best for the story he was telling. This naughty practice, adopted later by Macaulay, increased the literary effectiveness of the work: but to place the tale before the truth did not make better history. In any case his history has much of the *omnium gatherum* about it, with the trivial not sufficiently distinguished from the significant. We find indeed, that Gibbon, "unwearied with infinite detail", is lacking in a sense of proportion, and shows no proper selective judgment.

Many find the historian tedious because he expresses himself at such length, and the Abbé de Mably asks:* "Is there anything more wearisome than a Mr. Gibbon who, in his eternal history of the Roman emperors, suspends every instant his slow and insipid narrative to explain to you the causes of the events that you are going to read? Nothing ought to arrest me in a recital; and it must be clear—that is the first law for every historian; but it must be made so with an art that shall not repel me."

A famous Duke of Gloucester (1743-1805), when Gibbon presented him with one of his later volumes, welcomed it with the words, "Another damned, thick, square book! Always scribble, scribble, scribble! Eh! Mr. Gibbon?"

Gibbon may be said to come at the end of an epoch. His snobbish concentration on classical history shows that he was living in a highly artificial world, and was out of touch with the real life of his own country. The acceleration of the development of industry known as the Industrial Revolution is usually taken as dating from 1760, but Gibbon appears to have been quite unaware of the mighty forces at work around him when he planned the writing of his history in 1764. It is somewhat remarkable that the publication of the first part of the *Decline and Fall* in 1776 coincides with the appearance of the *Wealth of Nations* in the same year. What a contrast there was between Gibbon's outlook and that of Adam Smith. While a new science, a great literature, and a fresh interpretation of history have sprung from Adam Smith's work, there has been no major history of Rome since Gibbon's date, and none has been needed. A new history of Rome in six stout quarto volumes would today be quite unsaleable.

We have here the key to one of the most marked deficiencies of Gibbon's work. As economic science was quite outside his scope, he did not seek to treat the economic and intellectual problems of Roman decadence. The underlying social causes of change were neglected in favour of superficial political and other considerations. In this connection Morison remarks that: "The deep economic and social vices which undermined the great fabric—depopulation, decay of agriculture, fiscal oppression, the general prostration begotten of despotism—these considerations

* *De la manière d'écrire l'histoire*, 1783, pp. 217-218.

are not brought together to a luminous point. . . . They lie scattered, isolated, and barren over three volumes, and are easily overlooked. One may say that generalized and synthetic views are conspicuous by their absence in Gibbon."

Perhaps the greatest positive achievement of Gibbon is in tracing on natural principles the rise of Christianity, which he did comprehensively. This brought about a bond of sympathy between him and Hume. It showed also that the philosophers of France had played a decisive part in his intellectual development.

Accepting honestly the evidence about theology that his reading provided, the historian found himself obliged to discard earlier impressions. "Since my escape from Popery", he says, "I had humbly acquiesced in the common creed of the Protestant Churches; but in the latter end of the year 1759 the famous treatise of Grotius first engaged me in a regular trial of the evidence of Christianity. By every possible light that reason and history can afford, I have repeatedly viewed the important subject; nor was it my fault if I said with Montesquieu, 'Je lis pour m'édifier, mais cette lecture produit souvent en moi un effet tout contraire', since I am conscious to myself that the love of truth and the spirit of freedom directed my search."

Even in the first volume of his history Gibbon proceeds with his candid "enquiry into the *human* causes of the progress and establishment of Christianity". He has, in fact, from the beginning a clear conception of Christianity as a system that evolved. He was consequently attacked by clerical writers, especially by Richard Watson, afterwards Bishop of Llandaff, and found himself engaged in a literary controversy, publishing his *Vindication* to defend his own reasoning. Some years after his death there appeared *An Historical View of Christianity*, which he had written jointly with Voltaire, Bolingbroke and others.

The critical and commonsense attitude of Gibbon towards orthodox religion is well examplified by this passage on the basic doctrine of the immortality of the soul:

The writings of Cicero represent in the most lively colours the ignorance, the errors, and the uncertainty of the ancient philosophers with regard to the immortality of the soul. When they are desirous

of arming their disciples against the fear of death, they inculcate as
an obvious though melancholy position, that the fatal stroke of our
dissolution releases us from the calamities of life; and that those can
no longer suffer who no longer exist. Yet there were a few sages of
Greece and Rome who had conceived a more exalted, and in some
respects a juster idea of human nature; though it must be confessed,
that in the sublime inquiry, their reason had often been guided by
their imagination, and that their imagination had been prompted
by their vanity. When they viewed with complacency the extent of
their own mental powers; when they exercised their various faculties
of memory, of fancy, and of judgment, in the most profound speculations, or the most important labours; and when they reflected on
the desire of fame, which transported them into future ages, far beyond the bounds of death and of the grave; they were unwilling to
confound themselves with the beasts of the field, or to suppose that
a being, for whose dignity they entertained the most sincere admiration, could be limited to a spot of earth, and to a few years of duration. With this favourable prepossession, they summoned to their
aid the science, or rather the language of the metaphysics. They
soon discovered that as none of the properties of matter will apply to
the operations of the mind, the human soul must consequently be a
substance distinct from the body,—pure, simple and spiritual, incapable of dissolution, and susceptible of a much higher degree of virtue
and happiness after the release from its corporeal prison. From
these specious and noble principles, the philosophers who trod in the
footsteps of Plato deduced a very unjustifiable conclusion, since they
asserted not the future immortality, but the past eternity of the
human soul, which they were too apt to consider as a portion of the
infinite and self-existing spirit which pervades and sustains the
universe. A doctrine thus removed beyond the senses and the
experience of mankind might serve to amuse the leisure of a philosophic mind; or, in the silence of solitude, it might sometimes impart
a ray of comfort to desponding virtue; but the faint impression
which had been received in the school was soon obliterated by the
commerce and business of active life. We are sufficiently acquainted
with the eminent persons who flour 'ied in the age of Cicero, and
of the first Caesars, with their actions, their characters, and their
motives, to be assured that their conduct in this life was never
regulated by any serious conviction of the rewards or punishments
of a future state. At the bar and in the senate of Rome the ablest
orators were not apprehensive of giving offence to their hearers by
exposing that doctrine as an idle and extravagant opinion, which was
rejected with contempt by every man of a liberal education and
understanding.

It is amusing to note that the *Decline and Fall* had the honour of being bowdlerized by Bowdler himself, "with the careful omission of all passages of an irreligious or immoral tendency". Of the editions of the standard work, two of the best-known are those edited by Sir W. Smith in eight volumes, and by Professor J. B. Bury in seven volumes.

Charles Lamb did not like Gibbon's work. He includes the *Decline and Fall* in his catalogue of "books which are no books", but which are recommended by booksellers as being volumes which "no gentleman's library should be without". Lamb's friend Coleridge also had some severe things to say about the historian, including this passage:

Gibbon's style is detestable, but his style is not the worst thing about him. His history has proved an effectual bar to all real familiarity with the temper and habits of imperial Rome. . . . His work is little else but a disguised collection of all the splendid anecdotes which he could find in any book concerning any persons or nations from the Antonines to the capture of Constantinople. When I read a chapter in Gibbon, I seem to be looking through a luminous haze or fog; figures come and go, I know not how or why, all larger than life, or distorted or discoloured; nothing is real, vivid, true; all is scenical.

Mirabeau criticized Gibbon's "effeminate philosophy, which has more praise for luxury and pleasure than for all the virtues", and also his style, "always elegant and never energetic".

Of his style J. M. Robertson says that it is "always in stays, in ruffles, in processional robes. He seems to wave his hand and take snuff, with the fore-finger cocked (as was actually his habit), at every sentence; there is no gainsaying the charge that his writing is inveterately mannered, heavily periwigged, ceremoniously affected, as it were always in court dress." Burke termed his style "vicious and affected, deformed by too much literary tinsel and frippery". Another reference is to "the enamel of Gibbon's highly artificial style". Yet there is surely a refreshing, if somewhat gloomy directness of phrase when, for example, the historian says that, "the history of empires is the record of human misery", or that "history is indeed little more than the register of the crimes, follies, and misfortunes of mankind".

It seemed of interest to try to test if the *Decline and Fall* was maintaining its position, or whether any evidence was available to show that it was now read less than formerly. It appeared that one method of approach was to consider the editions published in fifty-year periods from 1800 to 1950. Below are given the numbers of editions held by the British Museum. While the figures are a reliable guide they are subject to certain reservations. Thus there is no evidence of the size of each edition. Further, it is necessary to bear in mind that copies of unaltered reprints need not be sent to the Museum under the Copyright Act. The figures are:

1800-1850	.	.	12
1850-1900	.	.	8
1900-1950	.	.	6

For two years after completing his history Gibbon did not seek any new task. Then, however, he began an account of the House of Brunswick. As he knew no German the choice was unwise, but in any event he was past serious work. He suffered from dropsy, and excessive fondness for sweet Madeira wine made him also subject to gout, so that he began to sink under his infirmities. Thus of the fresh project only the jejune Italian section was completed. His only important work apart from the *Decline and Fall* was, therefore, his *Autobiography*, of which his vanity caused him to write six separate versions, a record not yet equalled by anyone else.

Although permanently settled in Lausanne, the historian came to England in the latter part of 1793 to visit Lord Sheffield. Good living and lack of exercise had made him excessively corpulent, and the rigours of the journey worsened his dropsical condition. An operation gave some temporary relief, but he died in London in January 1794.

THE HISTORICAL WORK OF GIBBON
WITH DATES OF PUBLICATION

1776 *The Decline and Fall of the Roman Empire*, Vol. I.
1781 *The Decline and Fall of the Roman Empire*, Vols. II and III.
1788 *The Decline and Fall of the Roman Empire*, Vols. IV, V and VI.

CHAPTER VI

Robert Southey

(1774-1843)

ROBERT SOUTHEY was born at Bristol in August 1774, but his father came from the little country town of Wellington in Somerset, from which the Iron Duke afterwards derived his title. At the latter place the Southey family had been prominent since the fourteenth century, being engaged in sheep farming and in wool merchanting and manufacturing. Sheep had long been reared on the neighbouring Blackdown Hills, and Wellington itself is a woollen-making centre. Thomas Southey of the reign of Elizabeth, a direct ancestor of Robert the historian and poet, was one of the great clothiers of that beautiful corner of England. It was a tradition in the family that he "had eleven sons who peopled that part of the country with Southeys". A later Thomas Southey, wool broker, was the author in 1848 of *The Rise, Progress and Present State of Colonial Wools.*

Southey's great-grandfather, also named Robert Southey, lived at Wellington, and married Ann Locke, of the same family as the philosopher. Of his paternal stock the historian says: "They must have been of gentle blood, for they bore arms in an age when armorial bearings were not assumed by those who had no right to them. The arms are a cheveron *argent,* and three cross crosslets, *argent,* in a field *sable."* The heiress of an elder branch of the Southeys married Colonel the Hon. Hugh Somerville, and died in childbed of John Southey Somerville, afterwards 15th Lord Somerville, who was thus a cousin as well as a contemporary of the subject of this essay.

Much of Southey's childhood was spent with his aunt, Miss Tyler, a wealthy spinster who had a house in Bath. The residence stood in a walled garden, on the outskirts of the old city. Miss Tyler made certain alterations to the fabric, throwing two small rooms into one to make a good parlour, and building a drawing-room over the kitchen. In the drawing-room there hung her own portrait by Gainsborough, with a curtain to preserve the frame from flies and the colours from the sun. The

ROBERT SOUTHEY

from the portrait by John Opie

painting shows that there was a close resemblance between aunt and nephew. Also in this room were beautiful pieces of old furniture, including a cabinet of ivory, ebony, and tortoise-shell. The domestics of the establishment were an old man-servant and a maid, both of whom had been with their mistress for many years.

It was while living with his aunt that Southey went to his first day-school, and sometimes he accompanied her on visits to the home of his maternal grandfather at Bedminster. Of the main wainscotted apartment at Bedminster he says, "it was a cheerful room, with an air of such country comfort about it, that my little heart was always gladdened when I entered it during my grandfather's life. . . . The windows opened into the fore-court, and were as cheerful and fragrant in the season of flowers as roses and jessamine, which grew luxuriantly without, could make them."

The later school years of Southey were spent at Westminster, which he entered in April 1788. Simmons remarks that, "In Southey's day the school provided a severely classical education. Latin and Greek were not merely the chief subjects taught; they were almost the only ones—arithmetic was an extra subject taught by the writing-master on half holidays. Latin was the language of instruction in the Upper School; there were Latin 'themes' to be written; there was the 'Horace Lesson', which consisted in turning one of the Odes into a different metre from the original; it was Southey's inability to make Latin verses that automatically put him into a low form at his entrance."

The boy suffered many miseries at Westminster, and in later life often wrote denouncing the boarding-school system. His independent spirit and his keen intelligence were handicaps in an establishment then run on antiquated and rigidly stereotyped lines. Finally he was expelled in a way that was discreditable only to the headmaster, the latter discovering by underhand means that he was the author of an article criticizing flogging in a school magazine.

The choice had next to be made between further study at a university or entrance to some profession. He wrote about this time: "If I could get an appointment to the East Indies I should like it. The church is a hypocritical line of life, the law a dishonest one." Finally he chose the university, and entered

Oxford in January 1793. His father had died in the previous month, and his expenses at college were to be paid by his mother's brother, the Rev. Herbert Hill, British chaplain at Lisbon. This uncle had been at Christ Church, and Southey accordingly applied for admission there, but was refused because of the Westminster incident. The authorities at Balliol showed a little more sense, and he duly went into residence there.

Soon after his arrival at the university his tutor said to him: "Mr. Southey, you won't learn anything by my lectures; so, if you have any studies of your own, you had better pursue them." Southey afterwards declared that the only university studies he did pursue were swimming and boating. He disliked Oxford: "My college years were the least beneficial and least happy of my life", he wrote later. In his day most of the undergraduates were training to become clergymen. "We educate for only one profession," he remarked, "when colleges were founded that one was the most important; it is now no longer so; they who are destined for the others find it necessary to study elsewhere. This might be remedied. We have professors of everything, who hold their situations and do nothing. In Edinburgh, the income of the professor depends upon his exertions, and in consequence the reputation of that university is so high that Englishmen think it necessary to finish their education by spending a year there."

Southey left Oxford after being in residence for only about eighteen months. His uncle had pressed him to take orders, but to one of Southey's opinions to enter the church-gate was perjury, and although he wished to please his relatives the step was not possible. He tried the study of medicine but quickly gave it up because the dissecting-room filled him with unconquerable repugnance. Academic teaching did not appeal to him either, so that there was no object in remaining longer at the university.

Although Mr. Hill was naturally disappointed that his nephew felt unable to enter his own profession of the church, the relationship between them remained cordial. While Southey was deciding what occupation to take up, his uncle invited him to visit Spain and Portugal. The offer was too tempting to be refused, and from November 1795, the young man spent six happy months touring the Peninsula, learning the languages.

reading foreign poetry and history, and exploring among the books and manuscripts that Mr. Hill had collected in Lisbon: his future career was much influenced by this experience.

On this first visit he spent some time in Madrid while *en route* for Lisbon with Mr. Hill. He studied the Spanish language with enthusiasm, and soon had a fair acquaintance with its great writers. After the heat of Spain he found Lisbon a delightful spot, rejoicing in the mountains with their cool streams, the scents from the gardens, and the white breakers of the Atlantic. In April a move was made to a pleasant house Mr. Hill had at Cintra. These agreeable experiences gave Southey a strong impulse towards literary activity, and not only did he lay the foundations of his historical work at this time, but in 1797 he published his admirable *Letters written during a short Residence in Spain and Portugal*.

In the winter of 1799 Southey was very ill in Bristol with a nervous fever. When he was recovering his doctor advised a complete change of scene, and he longed to be at Cintra once more, with its perfumed lemon-groves and mountain grandeur. So when his ever generous uncle wrote inviting him to come again, he accepted eagerly, especially as there would be an opportunity of setting to work seriously on the *History of Portugal* which he already had ambitions to write. He sailed fom Falmouth in April 1800, this time accompanied by a young wife. This second visit lasted for nearly a year, and established firmly interests that remained with him for the rest of his life. He also reached an intellectual maturity in this period which might not have been his if he had been denied the benefits of travel and residence abroad.

A short stay was made in Lisbon before moving to Cintra. This enabled Southey to see the procession of the Body of God —he liked the English words as exposing "the naked nonsense of the blasphemy". In addition he went to a bull-fight, although he expected only to be pained and disgusted. He said afterwards that the bull-fight excited nothing but pain and anger at the cruelty and cowardice of the amusement.

At Cintra conditions were idyllic. In the evenings the fire-flies sparkled under the trees, until in July and August, when their light went out, the grillo began his song. "I eat oranges, figs, and delicious pears," wrote Southey, "drink Colares wine, a sort of half-way excellence between port and claret—read all I can lay my hands on—take a siesta of two hours, and am as happy as if life were but one everlasting today, and that tomorrow was not to be provided for."

But on the whole the season was by no means one of repose. Having quickly recovered his health, Southey rose at five to tackle folio after folio in his uncle's library, thus laying in "bricks for the great Pyramid of my history". Writing to a friend at this time he mentions, "The Portuguese chronicles, and the Spanish historians, of whom I shall peruse every one. Many of these it is needless to purchase. Many my uncle possesses. Still there is a heavy expenditure in indispensable books.' A good deal of his research was done in Lisbon, which was easily accessible. The main library there had much material which was useful to him, but he reported that, "the freedom of research is miserably shackled by the necessity of asking the librarian for every volume you wish to consult: to hunt a subject through a series of authors is thus rendered impossible". The old chronicles of the Portuguese Academy supplied him with the main facts, together with "a fair and accurate opinion of the chief personages, differing very considerably from their received characters". His intention was "to go through the chronicles in order, and then make a skeleton of the narrative". When he began the actual composition he wrote to his friend Wynn: "I hope you will like the plain, compressed, unornamented style, in which I endeavour to unite strength and perspicuity."

He obtained access to the library of Manuscripts in Lisbon, and wrote in this connection, "Of manuscripts, the most important are the five folio records of the Inquisition, in whose bloody annals the history of extinguished reformation must be sought. This is a somewhat awkward task. I have seen with eager eyes, itching fingers, and heretical qualms of apprehension this great mass, where and where only the documents for this very important period are attainable. The sub-librarian is an intelligent man—more eager to talk freely than I am to encourage the strain. He will not be alarmed to see me employed upon records which he abominates as religiously as myself."

One reason why Southey withheld publication of the *History of Portugal* as it progressed was because he feared that he had been too outspoken upon certain Church matters. He informed friends that he could publish nothing for the moment as his first volume would "touch popery to the quick", and that in consequence he would be denied access to Portuguese archives that he had still to explore. Probably he intended to publish the work as a whole, but we know that he never completed it. The issue was made more complex because in later life the reforming ardour of youth cooled. He did not abandon his Portuguese history altogether, however, and he was still endeavouring to finish it in the days when the labours of his pen finally came to an end.

In writing to one of his friends from Lisbon in December 1800, Southey gave this account of his work: "Historical researches, he says, "are very interesting, and of so varied a nature, that something may be done even in the most listless moment of indolence." He continues: "I should like, however, to indulge in an *amanuensis,* sit in an easy chair, screening my face from the fire with a folio, and so dictate in all imaginable ease. The contortions of the body from book to paper make my sides ache."

He made extensive journeys, through Portugal, and his knowledge of the countryside, the people and their customs all contributed to the background of his work. He travelled southwards to Algarve, and went northwards to Mafra to see the monastery and library there. "Do you love reading?" asked the friar who showed them round, when he overheard some reference to the books. "Yes, indeed!" replied Southey. "And I", retorted the candid Franciscan, "love eating and drinking." The well-stocked poultry-yard, the ducks on the monastic pond, and the other live-stock about the establishment suggested that adequate provision of this kind had been made.

Southey returned to England widely read, and with a good deal of material in hand for his history. Moreover he had acquired an intimate knowledge of just where other information was if he should ever return to complete his work in Portugal. It is a great pity that in point of fact he never did pay another visit to the Peninsula. Early in 1802 he settled in Bristol. Here he toiled at his history, taking a particular interest in the part relating to the religious orders. Books that he had collected in Lisbon arrived in packing-cases. "My dear and noble books!" he exclaimed. "Such folios of saints!" He soon had enough

books in England to keep him busily occupied for years. Some
of the works were dull but needed to be read to complete his
survey of the subject, even if it was shown subsequently that
they contained little of value. But as a rule his industry brought
him a great deal of pleasure: a folio yet untasted would jog his
elbow, and some of the best and rarest chronicles would invite
his attention. He traced the adventures of the great Constable
Nuño Alvares Pereyra, of King Joañ I, and of the Cid. And he
had the sporting pleasure of "hunting from their lair strange
facts about the orders Cistercian, Franciscan, Dominican,
Jesuit".

In 1803 Southey moved to the English Lake District, taking
up residence at Greta Hall, near Keswick, which remained his
home until his death nearly forty years later. The change was
made because his wife was expecting their first child, so that it
had become necessary to make suitable provision for family life.
In addition his great love of books made the permanent housing
of his rapidly growing collection a somewhat urgent matter:
his library at Greta Hall eventually held over 14,000 volumes.

The situation of Greta Hall can have few rivals for loveliness.
The mansion stands on an elevation by the river Greta, and was
surrounded by flower-bordered lawns, fruit trees and strawberry
beds. Beyond an orchard at the rear was a piece of woodland
reaching down to the stream. Here by the river was a rough
path, with a covered seat where Southey often came to sit and
read. From the grounds there were beautiful views of Derwent-
water and Bassenthwaite Lake, of Skiddaw and other neighbouring hills, and of Crosthwaite Old Church.

The interior of the house was equally attractive. As was
usual in eighteenth-century houses, some of the principal rooms
were on the first floor, this arrangement having the double
advantage of giving them additional quietness and privacy with
a more extensive outlook. Southey's neice, Sara Coleridge, says
that, "The stairs to the right of the kitchen led to a landing-
place filled with book-cases". Actually there do not appear to
have been many passages or corners free from books. "A few
steps farther", she continues, "was the study, where my uncle
sat all day occupied with literary labours and researches, but
which was used as a drawing-room for company. Here all the
tea-visiting guests were received. The room had three windows.

a large one looking down upon the green with the wide flower-border, and over to Keswick Lake and the mountains beyond. The room was lined with books in fine bindings. Altogether, with its noble outlook, and something pleasing in its proportions, this was a charming room."

Southey liked looking through books newly-arrived in that agreeable time of relaxation after the evening meal, while quietly enjoying a glass of his favourite currant-rum. "It would please you", he wrote to an old friend, "to see such a display of literary wealth, which is at once the pride of my eye, the joy of my heart, and the food of my mind; indeed, more than meta-phorically, meat, drink and clothes for me and mine. I verily believe that no-one in my station was ever so rich before, and I am very sure that no-one in any station had ever a more thorough enjoyment of riches of any kind or in any way." And it was indeed true that, apart from the great Heber library, his collection of Spanish and Portuguese works, both printed and in manuscript, was probably the finest belonging to any private person in the country.

From his library Southey abstracted materials for his work, forming gradually a very extensive series of transcripts. Dowden remarks that it is easy to perceive that the collector wrought under an historical bias, and that social, literary, and ecclesiastical history were the directions in which the historical tendency found its play. When Ticknor visited him in 1819 the young American was impressed by the great bundles of manu-script materials for the *History of Portugal,* and the *History of the Portuguese East Indies,* which Southey produced for his inspection. He was also charmed by the kindness of his recep-tion, by the air of culture and of goodness in the historian's home, and by Southey's bright and eager talk, "for the quickness of his mind expresses itself in the fluency of his utterance". In point of fact Southey liked company, and the pilgrimage to Greta to see him was made by many friends, often from distant parts of the country, and by distinguished scholars from the British universities, from the Continent and from America. "Old friends and old books", he said, "are the best things that this world affords (I like old wine also), and in these I am richer than most men (the wine excepted)." So his visitors—Sir Walter Scott, Wordsworth and the rest—were always welcome, however much they might interrupt the work upon which his livelihood depended.

To begin with Southey shared the attractive little domain of Greta with his brother-in-law Coleridge. Later he became the sole tenant of the estate, but through family circumstances he continued to support his sister-in-law and her children as well as his own growing brood. From 1807 he enjoyed a small government pension, but otherwise he had to earn with his pen all that was needed for his heavy domestic responsibilities. "To think", he exclaimed, "how many mouths I must feed out of one inkstand."

Southey had a good life at Greta, and his "temper and manners were full of a strong and sweet hilarity". A house in his view was not perfectly furnished for enjoyment unless it had in it a child rising three years old and a kitten rising six weeks, and he declared that "the kitten is in the animal world what the rosebud is in the garden". For many years there were in fact always plenty of both children and cats at Greta Hall. Among the latter was Lord Nelson, an ugly specimen of the ginger or streaked-carroty kind, yet withal a good cat, affectionate, vigilant and brave. The Admiral was succeeded by Madame Bianchi, a beautiful and singular creature, white with a fine tabby tail, whose "wild eyes were bright and green as the Duchess de Cadaval's emerald necklace". Then came almost together the never-to-be-enough-praised Rumpelstilzchen (afterwards raised for services against rats to be His Serene Highness the Archduke Rumpelstilzchen), and the equally-to-be-praised Hurlyburlypuss. What wonder that with such a household Southey should become the author of that children's classic *The Three Bears,* which forms, as it were, a perfect modern addition to our national folklore.

Under these happy and stable conditions Southey devoted himself to his literary work. Professor Dowden remarks that, "He grew stronger, calmer, more full-fraught with stores of knowledge, richer in treasure of the heart. . . . Everything is plain, straightforward, substantial. . . . What makes the life of Southey eminent and singular is its unity of purpose, its simplicity, purity, loyalty, fortitude, kindliness, truth." His industry was always exemplary, and Macaulay once wrote enviously: "There are people who can carry on twenty works at a time. Southey could write the *History of Brazil* before breakfast, an ode after breakfast, then the *History of the Peninsular War* till dinner, and an article for the *Quarterly Review* in the evening." The attitude of Southey himself is quite clear. "I feel", he said, "that duty and happiness are inseparable", and the record of his life shows how sincerely he held this conviction.

In his historical writings Southey has a crisp, straightforward style very much in keeping with an old and excellent English tradition. Coleridge says that "in the very best styles, as Southey's, you read page after page, understanding the author perfectly, without once taking notice of the medium of communication; it is as if he had been speaking to you all the while". But what appears as ease and clarity of expression to the reader almost inevitably demands much care and thought from the writer, and Southey found in maturity that he could not work quickly. "It is long", he says, "since I have been a rapid writer, and the pains which I take in collecting materials and making myself fully acquainted with the subject before me, render it impossible that I should be so. It is only by being never idle, when I can possibly be employed, that I am enabled to do much."

When his brother, Dr. Henry Southey, was thinking of writing something on the Crusades, Robert gave him some hints. "All relative matter", he wrote, "not absolutely essential to the subject, should go in the form of supplementary notes, and these you may make as amusing as you please, the more so, and the more curious, the better." Later in the same note he continues: "Omit none of those little circumstances which give life to narration, and bring old manners, old feelings, and old times before your eyes."

At the beginning of the nineteenth century there was growing public interest in South America. Mr. Hill returned home in 1801 after his long residence in Portugal. He brought with him his valuable collection of manuscript documents and other papers, containing a great deal of information about Portuguese colonial possessions, especially Brazil. This material he placed at the disposal of the Government, and, while no immediate use was made of it in official quarters, the offer led Lord Grenville to urge that it should be used as a basis for a history of Brazil, and Southey was readily persuaded to undertake the task.

The affection which Southey had for Portugal led him to take a deep interest in the empire that country had built up in Brazil. From the time that a Portuguese expedition discovered the Brazilian coast in 1500 there was the closest of links between the two countries until the colony declared its independence in 1822. Thus the connection had not been broken when Southey wrote his *History of Brazil*, the first volume of which appeared in 1810, the second in 1817, and the third and last in 1819. He was far-sighted enough to realize more fully than his contemporaries the splendid future that lay before Brazil, and foresaw the developments that even now are only gradually unfolding.

In a letter to a friend the historian wrote: "I am far from regretting that so much time and labour have been bestowed upon a subject for which few English readers can be expected to feel much interest. As long as I live I shall carefully correct and enlarge it from whatever documents, written or printed, may come to my hands, and centuries hence, when Brazil shall have become the great and prosperous country which one day it must be, I shall be regarded there as the first person who ever attempted to give a consistent form to its crude, unconnected and neglected history." With the exception of his *Life of Nelson*, this history is regarded as the best of Southey's prose works.

When the Southey Centenary Celebrations were opened at Keswick in August 1943, a notable tribute to the historian was paid by the Counsellor Minister of the Brazilian Embassy, Senhor Q. De Sousa Leão. He said that Southey in his history of Brazil wrote of a country he never saw, but whose greatness he foreshadowed, and his intuition that when Brazil became a great nation he would be remembered as the Herodotus of Brazil proved right. The history, which has remained the standard one on the subject in English, was first translated into Portuguese in 1862, a new translation being arranged in 1943. It is interesting to note that in February 1839, the Queen of Portugal created Southey a Knight of the Order of the Tower and Sword for his work on the history of Brazil.

This major work on the grand scale, for the *History of Brazil* was Southey's largest prose composition, brought only a small financial return, and this in spite of the fact that no one else in England could have written it. In the eight years after publication he received only as much from it as from one of his articles in the *Quarterly*.

The writing of the *History of Brazil* was a considerable literary feat, and Southey felt a good deal of pride in it. He was industrious in bringing together a great deal of factual information about the history of the country, and was skilful in arranging his material in an attractive way. There remained, however, the very serious disadvantage that Brazil, throughout the period covered by his narrative, was still a backward and primitive land without any great influence in world affairs. So, although the historian used his talents to full advantage, the events described do not lend themselves to dramatic effect, and are of interest mainly to the specialist.

The origin of Southey's famous *Life of Nelson* is to be found in an article on Nelson which he wrote for the *Quarterly Review* in 1810. The editor, Murray, saw at once the outstanding quality of the essay, and Southey not only received 20 guineas a sheet, or twice the usual rate of payment, but was immediately invited to expand the article into book form.

Three years were taken to write the book about Nelson, a work which came to be acknowledged as Southey's masterpiece. He spared no pains to see that all details were authentic, and was well aware of his own limitations as a landsman: "I am such a land lubber that I feel half ashamed of myself for being persuaded ever even to review the *Life of Nelson*, much more to write one. I walk among sea terms as a cat does in a china pantry, in bodily fear of doing mischief and betraying myself." Fortunately he was able to consult his brother, Commander Thomas Southey of the Royal Navy, who had fought at the battle of Copenhagen and who was extremely well informed about all matters relating to his profession. Apart from technical questions concerned with strategy and the like, his brother was called upon to note down particulars of vivid incidents of which he had been an eye-witness. In the course of a letter written to him on 30 December 1812, Southey says: "You used to speak of the dead lying in shoal water at Copenhagen; there was the boatswain's mate, or somebody, asked for, when he was lying face upward under the stern or somewhere. Tell me the right particulars of this, which is too striking a circumstance to be lost."

By combining close attention to accuracy with a powerful imagination that enabled him to relive the incidents of Nelson's campaigns, Southey succeeded in presenting an inspired portrait of the Admiral. Once again Nelson paced his quarter-deck, spoke and had his being. The popular conception of this national hero which we have today is derived very largely from Southey's work. The value of the biography depends on the application of the author's literary genius to historical truth. It has been said that, "Southey wrote of the fullness of know-ledge; and his was that rarest gift of good pure English. *The Life of Nelson* belongs to universal literature. It remains a classic, because no biographer was ever more in sympathy with his hero or wrote more simply and directly." Sir Humphry Davy called this work, "an immortal monument raised by genius to valour". In this book Southey's clear, masculine English is seen at its best—"sinewy and flexible, easy and melodious".

A specially luxurious edition of the Nelson biography was published in 1911. In an introduction to this John Masefield suggests that Southey in describing Nelson's naval achievements did not always do full justice to the peculiar intellectual power exercised before, during and after them, in that the results he obtained in battle came from a very special faculty of mind strengthened by unceasing meditation upon tactical problems. Nelson's instinct for war was unerring; but no naval officer of his generation gave more thought to the application of that instinct. His brain was burningly busy night and day with the problem, "How to smash the enemy if he come thus, or thus, or thus".

The project of the *History of Portugal* was conceived on the grandest scale when Southey was twenty-six. It was intended quite seriously to rival Gibbon's history, and might well have done so. The record of the Portuguese empire in Brazil was part of this great scheme. Otherwise the only fragment pub-lished was that masterpiece of narrative, *The Expedition of Orsua, and the Crimes of Aguirre,* which appeared in 1821. In August 1822, Southey wrote that his Portuguese history was practically complete down to the accession of Don Sebastian in 1557, but it never saw the light.

Doubtless it is no accident that the *History of Portugal* was never published. At bottom Southey was always conventional in outlook, resembling in later years his ultra-respectable old aunt at Bath. As fame, position, public esteem and the conservatism of old age became increasingly his lot, to publish would have been to risk social suicide, having regard to the religious views expressed, the vigour of which we can gauge from his commonplace book. Then again his only son to reach maturity became a clergyman, and one of his two surviving daughters married a minister, so that if he did not deal with his manuscript during his lifetime they would know what to do with it afterwards. It is unlikely that he would destroy the child of his own brain, even if he lacked the courage to publish, and in fact his son-in-law stated that the manuscript, with additional material, was in his possession. It is more likely, therefore, that his heirs, in a mistaken view of what was due to his memory, chose not to preserve this work, although he himself may well have hoped that it would be published posthumously. In any event it seems clear that there is really no mystery of a missing manuscript, and that we cannot expect anything to be discovered and published now.

It is comparatively rare for two historians to choose the same specialized theme, but this did happen with Southey and Sir William Napier. Southey's *History of the Peninsular War* was published in three volumes between 1823 and 1832. Napier's *History of the War of the Peninsula* followed in six volumes between 1828 and 1840. The character of the two men is so entirely different, and their approach to the subject so opposed, that although they were great rivals their works were largely complementary to each other: to obtain a complete picture of the campaign both histories must be read.

General Napier was a choleric military man of decided views and fixed opinions. He seems to have been a keen partisan, vigorously defending any cause in which he believed, and making something of a hobby of literary controversy. In his book he was much concerned with a vindication of Wellington and Sir John Moore. He wrote as a soldier who had taken part in the actions described, and limited himself to the British point of view simply because he was unaware that any other existed.

Southey, on the other hand, was a man of letters working quietly in his library. His early associations with the Peninsula made him anxious to do full justice to the courage and other virtues of the people of Spain. In this he may have been over-generous, but at least he was most conscientious in consulting sources, examining manuscripts, and corresponding with eye-witnesses. In this connection Dowden remarks that it may be that enduring spiritual forces became apparent to the distant observer which were masked by the accidents of the day and hours from one like Napier who was in their midst.

Historians are not always kind to one another, and sometimes differences of opinion may be harshly termed errors by rivals in the craft. Thus Napier, when admitting a mistake in his own book, made the gratuitous and malicious comment that it "was not drawn from Mr. Southey's history, though I readily acknow-ledge I could not go to a more copious source of error".

In his essays in the *Quarterly Review* Southey expresses firmly some of his long-held opinions. Superstition, which he had seen as the chief spiritual food of Spain, made him a determined opponent of Catholicism. He held that Catholic Emancipation would not reconcile Ireland, and that it was the responsibility of the English to educate the people of Ireland, to execute justice there, and to maintain peace. He wrote to a friend: "You wrong the Government with regard to Ireland. They neither now have, nor ever have had, a wish to keep the savages in that country in their state of ignorance and barbarity; and it would surprise you to know what funds have been established for their education. *How* to set about enlightening such a people as the wild Irish is one of the most difficult duties any government was ever called upon to perform, obstructed as it is by such a body of priests, who can effectually prevent any better instruc-tion than they themselves bestow."

Southey was accorded many of the forms of recognition appropriate to his literary eminence. Oxford gave him a Doctorate of Civil Law. Cambridge, too, offered him an honorary degree, but he declined it. We know that he was an austere man, but such a refusal savours of unreasonable dis-courtesy and lack of appreciation towards those showing him kindness. There was other evidence of this trait: thus when the Royal Society of Literature presented him with a gold medal, he was cold-blooded enough to change it promptly for a silver coffee-pot for Mrs. Southey, something which he could quite well have afforded to buy her in any case. He was, in fact, rather forbiddingly arrogant in such matters.

In 1833 he was asked to stand for the post of Professor of History in the newly constituted University of Durham, but would not leave Keswick. Peel wrote offering him a baronetcy, the King having already consented. This honour Southey refused, not because he disliked the idea, but because he thought he might be expected to live at a higher rate than before. He had become well-placed financially, but he was constitutionally cautious, and was intent upon building up the moderate fortune which he eventually left to his family. His earnings were fairly high. For his regular articles in the *Quarterly* he received £100 apiece. The history of the *Peninsular War* brought him £1,000, although the copyright remained the publisher's property. The rate paid for the several volumes of two editions of the *Naval History* is variously stated as 500 guineas or £750 a volume. He became adept, in fact, at playing off one publishing house against another. Again for editing Cowper's works, and providing a short biography, he earned a fee of 1,000 guineas.

He died in March 1843, and was buried in the ancient Crosthwaite village church near his Lakeland home. The church has become a place of pilgrimage, half hidden by stately old trees. It was natural that his final resting place should be here, but memorials were erected also in Westminster Abbey and in Bristol Cathedral.

THE HISTORICAL WORKS OF SOUTHEY
WITH DATES OF PUBLICATION

1797   *On the French Revolution, by Jacques Necker*, Vol. II translated by Southey from the French.

1808   *The Chronicle of the Cid*, translated by Southey from the Spanish.

1810-19   *The History of Brazil*.

1813   *The Life of Nelson*.

1821   *The Expedition of Orsua*, being an Episode from the otherwise unpublished *History of Portugal*.

1823-32   *History of the Peninsula War*.

1833-40   *Lives of the Admirals*, or *The Naval History of England*.

1844   *Biography of Cromwell* (published posthumously).

CHAPTER VII

William Hickling Prescott
(1796–1859)

THE lives of some men merit special admiration because they accomplish great work under conditions of peculiar hardship or difficulty. In particular, genius manifesting itself in spite of severe physical disability and suffering deserves our sympathetic wonder. Prescott was afflicted in early youth with partial blindness, but nevertheless rejected the life of ease that his ample means made possible, and devoted himself unsparingly to the exacting work of historical research. His career is a striking example of what can be done by courage and perseverance even when circumstances are at their worst.

The Prescott family were of the original Puritan stock of New England. William Hickling Prescott, born in Salem, Massachusetts, on 4 May 1796, was sixth in descent from John Prescott, a Lancashire man who left England about 1640 and established himself in Massachusetts only twenty years after the first settlement. The family no doubt sprang originally from the town of Prescot, near Liverpool in Lancashire.

The father of the historian, Judge Prescott, hoped his son would also follow the legal profession. With this object in view the son received the classical education traditional in the family. At the age of twelve he was placed under the Rev. Dr. Gardiner of Boston, who received about a dozen youths to study the Greek and Latin classics. Young Prescott formed a strong attachment for Dr. Gardiner, and many years afterwards his old tutor, during his long-protracted last illness, directed his servant to admit no one except his family connections and Mr. Prescott.

When Prescott entered Harvard it is said that, thanks to Dr. Gardiner, he probably knew more of Latin and Greek than many students did by the time they graduated. He had a strong dislike for mathematics, a subject which, but for his exceptional memory, might have proved a serious obstacle in his academic career. In his first year there occurred an accident which cost him the sight of one eye and gravely impaired that

W. H. PRESCOTT

from the drawing by George Richmond

of the other. He was absent from the university for a time, and when he returned his sufferings had sobered him beyond his years. It was difficult for him to continue his studies, but his never-failing courage enabled him to do so, and he was graduated with some of the customary honours of successful scholarship.

Upon leaving college Prescott began to read for the bar. He still lingered fondly over his Greek and Latin books, and was encouraged in an indulgence of his preference by his family and friends, who regarded these studies as a suitable path to forensic eminence. After a few months, however, intense inflammation of his remaining eye set in. Power of vision was completely lost for several days, and he lay in a fever from which there seemed little hope of recovering. When at last he recovered, it was found that the cause of the trouble with the eye was a form of acute rheumatism which permanently affected the retina. For periods of several years at a time no reading or writing was possible. The legal career had consequently to be abandoned. It is infinitely to his credit that, although sometimes totally blind, Prescott made his life rich in interest and strong in purpose. In training himself for his task as a historian, as for example in his study of languages, and in his intense and laborious research into the original documents relating to the particular branches of history that attracted him, he was obliged to adopt stern self-discipline and a monotonous regularity of existence in order to overcome his disabilities. Prescott was extremely thorough in the preparation of his material, and most painstaking as a writer.

On a visit to London in 1816, when twenty years of age, he placed himself in the hands of Sir William Adams, a famous oculist, who confirmed the opinion of former advisers that his case admitted of no remedy. While in Europe he visited Turin, Milan, Venice, Florence and Rome; spent a month in Naples; and went to see General Lafayette in Paris. In England he spent some time listening to debates in the Houses of Lords and Commons and paid visits to Oxford and Cambridge. The following year was notable for the appearance in the *North American Review* of his first published article.

The historian married when twenty-four, having been fortunate in finding an ideal helpmate. The couple had an intimate friend of George Ticknor, who says of them: "If there was ever a devoted wife, or a tender and grateful husband, they were to be found in the home which this union made happy." Prescott himself wrote long afterwards: "Contrary to the assertion of La Bruyère—who somewhere says that the most fortunate husband finds reason to regret his condition at least once in twenty-four hours—I may truly say that I have found no such day in the quarter of a century that Providence has spared us to each other." And so it was to the end.

History was bound up a little in the marriage. The grand-fathers of the historian and his wife had fought on opposite sides in the War of American Independence: Colonel Prescott held a command at Bunker's Hill, and Captain Lindsay, of the sloop-of-war *Falcon,* cannonaded him and his redoubt from the waters of the Charles river. The swords worn on this memorable occasion by both the army officer and the naval officer were treated as heirlooms in their respective families, till they came to be crossed peacefully above the books in Prescott's library. At his death they were transferred at his desire to the Historical Society of Massachusetts. Perhaps these old trophies may be taken as encouraging evidence of the transitory nature of human animosities.

For some years Prescott studied English, French and Italian literature, only his infirmity of sight preventing him from adding German. Part of his remarkable power over language must certainly have resulted from his wide reading. His earliest literary studies in adult life were naturally in his mother tongue, beginning with Ascham, Sir Philip Sidney, Bacon, Browne, Ralegh and Milton; but he continued to devote a fixed part of each day to the Latin classics, especially Tacitus, Livy, and Cicero. It was a natural step from Latin to French literature, though the latter never greatly attracted him. He had the remarkable ambition of forming an acquaintance with the whole of French literature from Froissart to Chateaubriand. He found, however, that it did not satisfy him as English had done, and that it was less rich, vigorous and original. He enjoyed Montaigne and admired Pascal, but gave wholehearted respect only to La Fontaine and Molière. French poetry, and the rigorous system of rhymes enforced in its tragedies, he disliked.

After French came the more serious question, so far as

Prescott was concerned, of Italian. He read first such books as would make him most quickly familiar with the language, and turned to Sismondi's *Littérature du Midi* to obtain an outline of the whole field. Italian literature made a deep impression on him, and for a time he thought of devoting his life to the study of it. The richness and perfection of the Italian in the hands of Petrarch he found truly wonderful, and he held the view that he had never read a foreign poet who possessed more of the spirit of the best English poetry.

Enjoyment of Dante inevitably came with increasing knowledge of Italian. To his mind the most conspicuous quality of Dante was simplicity, and in this he thought this author's works superior to any other he had ever read, with the possible exception of some parts of the Scriptures. It seemed to Prescott that the *Inferno* consisted of a series of pictures of the most ingenious, the most acture, and sometimes the most disgusting bodily sufferings. He wished, however, that Dante had made more use of the *mind* as a source and a means of anguish. He felt that, in general, the sufferings inflicted were purely physical. He regarded Dante's devils and bad spirits, with one or two exceptions, as much inferior in moral grandeur to Milton's. To his mind the stupendous, overgrown Satan of the *Inferno* could not compare with the sublime spirit of Milton's, not yet stripped of all its original brightness. He looked upon the *Purgatorio*, full of sober meditation and sweet description, as more *a l'Anglaise* than any other part of the *Commedia*. In addition to reading the *Divine Comedy* in the original Prescott made use of Cary's translation, which he held in high esteem. He once expressed the opinion that if Dante could have foreseen Carey's translation, he would have given the translator a place in his ninth heaven. He found it most astonishing, giving not only the literal corresponding phrase, but the spirit of the original, and thought it should be cited as evidence of the compactness, the pliability, the sweetness of the English tongue. He observed that it was a triumph of our mother tongue to be able to express every idea of the most condensed original in the Latin tongue in a smaller compass in this translation—Cary's cantos being generally five or six lines shorter than Dante's.

A series of lectures by his friend Ticknor, who had become Professor of Spanish Literature at Harvard University, first awakened Prescott's enthusiasm for Spanish history, and caused him to devote two years to the study of Spanish. Then, in 1826, at the age of thirty, he began the *History of the Reign of Ferdinand and Isabella*, which was to occupy him for ten years.

When he received from Madrid some of the early materials for the *History of Ferdinand and Isabella*, the historian, in his disabled condition, with his transatlantic treasures around him, felt like one pining from hunger in the midst of abundance. He resolved to make the ear do the work of the eye. Obtaining the services of a university graduate as secretary to read the various authorities to him, he became in time so familiar with the sounds of the different foreign languages that he could understand the reading without much difficulty. The historian mentions that the doubtful orthography and defiance of all punctuation in the manuscripts were so many stumbling blocks to his amanuensis. As his secretary proceeded, he dictated copious notes, which in turn were read to him repeatedly till he had mastered their contents sufficiently for the purpose of composition.

Another difficulty, arising in the mechanical labour of writing, was remedied by means of a writing-case, such as is used by the blind, which enabled him to commit his thoughts to paper without the aid of sight, serving him equally well in the dark as in the light. Prescott comments that the characters thus formed were little different from hieroglyphics, but that his secretary became expert in deciphering them. Finally, a fair copy was made for the use of the printer. What a boon the modern typewriter would have been in these circumstances.

Prescott was aware of the extreme importance of the reign of Ferdinand and Isabella. In it the several states into which Spain had previously been divided—Castile, Aragon and Granada—were for the first time brought under a common rule; America was discovered and colonized; the ancient empire of the Spanish Arabs was subdued; the dread tribunal of the Inquisition was established; and the Jews, who had contributed so much to the wealth and civilization of the country, were banished. Yet in spite of the significance of these events, no earlier historian had chosen this period for study. Prescott

realized, too, that these changes formed the basis of the remarkable careers of Charles V and Philip II, about which he was
afterwards to write. Three and a half years after the selection
of his subject he began actual composition, and found much
satisfaction in his work without having more than very moderate
expectations from it. Seven years later the book was ready for
publication, and he was anxious about its reception by the
public. His fears were groundless, for the work was at once
popular, the first edition being exhausted in five weeks.

Of this work he remarked: "I have made a book illustrating
an unexplored and important period, from authentic materials,
obtained with much difficulty and probably in the possession
of no one library, public or private, in Europe. As a plain,
veracious record of facts, the work, therefore, till someone else
shall be found to make a better one, will fill up a gap in literature
which, I should hope, will give it a permanent value—a value
founded on its utility, though bringing no great fame or gain
to its author." He confessed that because of the state of his eyes
he had often studied with little spirit and little expectation of
being able to carry the work to completion.

Prescott made some notes on style which are of interest.
We are reminded of Hume when he says, "Unless something is
gained in the way of strength or of colouring, it is best to use
the most simple, *unnoticeable* words to express ordinary things;
for example, 'to send' is better than 'to transmit'; crown
'descended' better than crown 'devolved'; guns 'fired' than guns
'discharged'; 'to name' or 'call' than 'to nominate'; 'to read' than
'to peruse'; 'the term' or 'name' than 'apellation', and so forth.
It is better also not to encumber the sentence with long, lumber-
ing nouns; as, 'the relinquishment of' instead of 'relinquish-
ing'; 'the embellishment and fortification of' instead of 'em-
bellishing and fortifying'; and so forth." To the end of his
life he continued to correct his composition with care and
severity.

He was naturally concerned with style in the case of his
earlier work, before he gained experience and confidence. Before
the *Ferdinand and Isabella* history was published, he wrote this
note about it: "With regard to the style of this work, I will
only remark that most of the defects, such as they are, may be
comprehended in the words *trop soigné*. The only rule is, to

write with freedom and nature, even with homeliness of expression occasionally. If the sentiment is warm, lively, forcible, the reader will be carried along without much heed to the arrangement of the periods. Put life into the narrative, if you would have it take. Elaborate and artificial fastidiousness in the form of expression is highly detrimental to this. A book may be made up of perfect sentences and yet the general impression be very imperfect. In fine, be engrossed with the thought and not with the fashion of expressing it."

In writing his *Ferdinand and Isabella* the historian naturally expressed a great deal not only of himself but of his period and nationality. He himself was a product of the American democracy, and was open-minded and unbiased in both political and religious matters. The same reasoning applies with equal force to his later works. In Europe, on the other hand, and especially in a Catholic country like Spain, the outlook of people was more conservative. So when *Ferdinand and Isabella* was translated into Spanish by Saban, the translator added notes which showed a marked divergence of thought between him and the author. Prescott makes this comment in a letter to his friend Don Pascual de Gazangos: "The translation appears faithful, as far as I have compared it. As to its literary execution in other respects, a foreigner cannot decide. But I wish you would give my thanks to the translator for the pleasure it has given me. His notes on the whole are courteous, though they show that Señor Saban has contemplated the ground often, from a different point of view from myself. But this is natural. For am I not the child of democracy? Yet no bigoted one, I assure you. I am no friend to bigotry in politics or religion, and I believe that forms are not so important as the manner in which they are administered. The mechanical execution of the book is excellent. It gives me real pleasure to see myself put into so respectable a dress in Madrid. I prize a translation into the noble Castilian more than any other tongue." It may be noticed that translations into French, Italian and German quickly followed the Spanish one.

The author was delighted with his success, and took a year's holiday in which to enjoy it. He became popular in society, having a charming personality. Premature decay of his remaining eye had now set in, making work more difficult, but he soon began to plan his next book. Thoughts of a life of Molière were given up in favour of another Spanish subject. Prescott's imagination was struck by the achievement of the handful of Spanish adventurers who undertook and carried out the conquest of the empire of Mexico. In his forty-third year he began his history of this undertaking.

Crates of books and manuscripts were sent from Mexico and Spain, and the work was well in hand when Prescott heard that Washington Irving had the same theme in view for a sequel to his *Columbus*. Irving retired with magnanimity in favour of the younger man, and in a letter to him said: "In at once yielding the thing to you, I feel that I am but doing my duty in leaving one of the most magnificent themes in American history to be treated by one who will build up from it an enduring monument in the literature of our country."

Prescott found the British Museum much richer in materials than he had anticipated, particularly in the number of chronicles and memoirs. Concerning this type of source he wrote: "I have always found a good, gossiping chronicle or memoir the best and most fruitful material for the historian. Official documents, though valuable on other accounts, contain no private relations; nothing, in short, but what was meant for the public eyes. Even letters of business are very apt to be cold and general. But a private correspondence like Peter Martyr's, or a chronicle like Pulgar's or Bernal Diaz's, is a jewel of inestimable price. There is nothing so serviceable to the painter of men and manners of a distant age."

The writing of the *Conquest of Mexico* took five years. The first part was the most difficult, since it necessarily dealt with the early traditions and history of Mexico, including much relating to its curious civilization both before and during the Conquest. Prescott found that most of what had passed for learning on the subject was, from his more accurate point of view, "mist and moonshine speculations". The great outstanding figure of the work, drawn with consummate skill by the historian, is Hernando Cortes, who entered on the conquest of a civilized nation and vast country with a force of only five hundred and fifty Spaniards, twelve horses, and ten brass guns.

It is generally considered that Prescott's style reached its happiest development in his *Conquest of Mexico*. The freshness and freedom of his descriptions of scenery, battles and marches have rendered the style singularly attractive. His style is specially well suited to the romantic subject of his work.

The *Conquest of Mexico* was published in 1843, and five thousand copies were sold in the first four months. The great success of the work, besides giving its author an international reputation, encouraged him to go forward with his *Conquest of Peru*, for which his researches had already provided ample matter. Prescott was fifty when he finished it, and, through decay of the nerve, the power of his eye was gradually becoming less. He was able to use it for only one hour a day, and that divided into two parts with a long interval between.

Prescott paid his second visit to Europe when fifty-four, and visited England, Scotland, France, Belgium and Holland. He was given a great reception in England, which he saw at the height of the Victorian prosperity, and London society made much of him. From the letters to his wife and daughter which friends or a private secretary wrote from his dictation, because the condition of his eye would not allow him to write himself, we get a very intimate impression of his day to day experiences. The atmosphere of what can now be seen as a well-defined era is strikingly revealed. What he wrote merely as casual gossip for the members of his family has acquired historical and social interest with the passage of time, the more so as it was written by so intelligent and informed an observer.

During his stay he met many interesting people. Of Macaulay he said: "I have met him several times. His memory for quotations and illustration is a miracle—quite disconcerting. He comes to a talk like one specially crammed. Yet you may start the topic. His talk is like the laboured, but still unintermitting, jerks of a pump."

He was impressed by the great Duke of Wellington, of whom he said: "I saw an old gentleman, stooping a good deal, very much decorated with orders, and making his way easily among us all; young and old seemed to treat him with deference. It was the Duke—the old Iron Duke. He is a striking figure. His aquiline nose is strongly cut, and his large forehead has but few wrinkles. He does not show the wear and tear of time and thought, and his benevolent expression has all the *iron* worked out of it. His face is fresh as a young man's. It is interesting to see with what an affectionate and respectful feeling he is regarded by all—not least by the Queen." At this time the Duke was in his eighty-second year. This historian records his reply to a lady who was glorifying his victories. "A victory, ma'am," said the Iron Duke, "is the saddest thing in the world, except a defeat."

In London the visitor was presented at Court, and wrote: "Do you know, by the way, that I have become a courtier, and affect the royal presence? I wish you could see my gallant costume—gold-laced coat, white inexpressibles, silk hose, gold-buckled patent slippers, sword and chapeau, etc. Am I not playing the fool as well as my betters?"

One of the people that Prescott visited was the Duke of Northumberland, at Alnwick Castle: "He is a good-looking man, with light hair, blue eyes, rather tall, frank and cordial in his manners. He has been a captain in the Navy." Forty people sat down to dinner. . . . "There was a multitude of servants, and the liveries—blue, white and gold—of the Duke, were very rich. We had also our own servants to wait on us. The table was loaded with silver. Every plate was silver, and everything was blazoned with the Northumberland Arms." After this display of extravagance, of a kind which is now without parallel in a private establishment, the company adjourned to the drawing room, "hung round with full-length portraits of the Duke's ancestors, some of them in their robes of state, very showy", for a concert by musicians brought specially from London. "Finally", says the historian, "I went to bed in a circular room in one of the towers, with a window, shaped something like a rose, set into a wall from five to six feet thick." Waking next morning to hear the deep tones of an old clock striking seven, he adds, "As I looked out of the window, I saw myself to be truly in an old baronial fortress, with its dark walls and towers gloomily mustered around it. On the turrets, in all directions, were stone figures of men, as large as life, with pikes, battle axes, etc., leaning over the battlements, apparently in the act of defending the castle—a most singular effect."

A few days later he called at Naworth Castle and enjoyed a game dinner of grouse and blackcock shot on the neighbouring moor. The meal was served in the long hall, with its fine old portraits. A great fire blazed in the hall; "The chimney, which has a grate to correspond, is full twelve feet in breadth; a fine old baronial chimney, at which they roasted whole oxen, I suppose."

Later the historian stayed at Castle Howard at the same time as Queen Victoria. Again there was a formal dinner. "It was a brilliant show, I assure you—that immense table with its fruit and flowers, and light glancing over beautiful plate, and in that superb gallery. I was as near the Queen as at our own family table. She has a good appetite and laughs merrily. She has fine eyes and teeth, but is short. She was dressed in black silk and lace, with the blue scarf of the Order of the Garter across her bosom." The constant feasting caused him to put on weight. In the country he was given a good deal of mutton, and remarked to Lord Carlisle: "Instead of John Bull, the Englishman should be called John Mutton, for he eats beef only one day in the week, and mutton the other six."

He went to Oxford to receive the degree of Doctor of Civil Law, staying the night before at Cuddesden Palace, the mansion seven miles from the city occupied from ancient times by the Bishops of Oxford. At such places he could see the English scene at its best: "My bedroom looks out on a lawn, dotted with old trees, over whose tops the rooks are sailing and cawing, while a highly gifted nightingale is filling the air with his melody." He gives this account of the actual degree ceremony: "Lord Northampton* and I were Doctorized in due form. We were both dressed in flaming red robes (it was the hottest day I have felt here). Professor Phillimore made a long Latin exposition of our merits, in which each of the adjectives ended, as Southey said in reference to himself on a like occasion, in *issimus*. We lunched with the Vice-Chancellor, who told me I should have had a degree on Commemoration day, the regular day; but he wrote about me to the Dean of St. Paul's, who was absent from town, and so an answer was not received until too late. He did not tell me that the principal object of the letter was to learn my faith, having some misgivings as to my heresy."

Prescott, having a frank and open nature, did not conceal his satisfaction at receiving the Oxford Doctorate. More than one American university had already bestowed an honorary

---

*The then Marquis of Northampton was at this time President of the Royal Society.

degree upon him, but he was well aware how lavishly the colleges of his own country then conferred their favours, and it pleased him that he was "now a real Doctor" as he expressed it. He was pleased, also by the kindly reception he received here and elsewhere in England and Scotland, and said: "They treat me, one and all, as if I was one of themselves. What can be so grateful to the wanderer in a foreign land as to find himself at once among friends?"

While Prescott was in Britain he had an excellent opportunity of studying the characteristics of our aristocracy. Of our national character he said: "It is full of generous, true and manly qualities and I doubt if there ever was so high a standard of morality in an aristocracy which has such means of self-indulgence at its command, and which occupies a position that secures it so much deference. There never was an aristocracy which combined so much practical knowledge and industry with the advantages of exalted rank."

The historian continues: "The Englishman is the most truly rural in his tastes and habits of any people in the world. I am speaking of the higher classes. The aristocracy of other countries affect the camp and the city. But the English love their old castles and country seats with a patriotic love. They are fond of country sports. Every man shoots or hunts. No man is too old to be in the saddle some part of the day, and men of seventy years and more follow the hounds and take a five-barred gate at a leap. The woman are good whips, are fond of horses and dogs and other animals. Duchesses have their cows, their poultry, their pigs—all watched over and provided with accommodations of Dutch-like neatness. All this is characteristic of the people. It may be thought to detract from the feminine graces which, in other lands, makes a woman so amiably dependent as to be nearly imbecile. But it produces a healthy and blooming race of women to match the hardy Englishmen—the finest development of the physical and moral nature which the world has witnessed. For we are not to look on the English gentleman as a mere Nimrod. With all his relish for field sports and country usages, he has his house filled with collections of art and with extensive libraries. The tables of the drawing-rooms are covered with the latest works sent down by the London publisher . . . with all their faults, never

has the sun shone—if one may use the expression in reference
to England—on a more noble race, or one that has done more
for the great interests of humanity." A very pleasant tribute to
come from a good American friend of this country. There are
other indications of how closely Prescott observed the people
he met here, as when he says: "There is a depth in the English
character, and at the same time a constitutional reserve, sometimes amounting to shyness, which it requires some degree of
intimacy to penetrate."

The historian wrote various critical and historical essays, a
number of which were selected for publication in book form in
1845. Among them was one on Scottish Song, in which an
interesting comparison is made between the ballads of Scotland
and Spain. Other essays were on Molière, Chateaubriand and
Sir Walter Scott. In considering early Scottish poetry Prescott
was struck by the fact that verse, which is esteemed so much
more difficult than prose among cultivated people, should uni-
versally have been the form which man, in the primitive stages
of society, adopted for the easier development of his ideas. He
suggests that nations in their infancy, like individuals, may be
more occupied with imagination and sentiment than with
reasoning, being thus led instinctively to verse, as best suited,
by its sweetness and harmony, to the expression of passionate
thought. It may be, of course, that the refinements of modern
criticism have multiplied rather than relieved the difficulties
of art. The ancient poet perhaps had little thought beyond
fitting his verses to the natural music of his own ear, free
from the strict observances which our more artificial age
demands.

Of the later poets of Scotland he says of Burns that his
universal genius seems to have concentrated within itself the
rays which were scattered among his predecessors—the simple
tenderness of Crawford, the fidelity of Ramsay, and the careless
humour of Ferguson. Prescott very happily remarks that it is
impossible to trace the authors of the majority of the popular
lyrics of Scotland, which, like its native flowers, seem to have
sprung up spontaneously in the most sequestered solitudes of
the country.

Prescott showed a more than ordinary interest in other
things Scottish, perhaps because of his wife's Lindsay ancestry.

But this did not cause him to lose his critical faculty. He writes, for example: "I return you Carlyle with my thanks. I have read as much of him as I could stand. After a very candid desire to relish him, I must say I do not at all. I think he has proceeded on a wrong principle altogether. The French Revolution is a most lamentable comedy (as Nick Bottom says) of itself, and requires nothing but the simplest statement of facts to freeze one's blood. To attempt to colour so highly what nature has already overclouded is, it appears to me, in very bad taste, and produces a grotesque and ludicrous effect, the very opposite of the sublime or beautiful."

Prescott's last two works were histories of Charles V, after his abdication from the throne of Spain, and of his son Philip II. Two volumes of Philip appeared first, in 1855, then the account of Charles in 1856, followed by the third Philip volume in 1858. In August 1854, Prescott made his *Philip the Second* the subject of a memorandum of which the following is an abstract: "By next spring, when I trust these volumes will be published, nearly eight years will have elapsed since the publication of the *Conquest of Peru*, which was also in two volumes, and which was published in less than four years after the appearance of the *Conquest of Mexico*. The cause of this difference is to be charged even more on the state of my eyes than on the difficulty and extent of the subject. For a long time after the *Peru* was published I hardly ventured to look into a book, and though I have grown bolder as I have advanced, my waning vision has warned me to manage my eye with much greater reserve than formerly. Indeed, for some time after I had finished the *Peru*, I hesitated whether I should grapple with the whole subject of *Philip in extenso;* and, when I made up my mind to serve up the whole barbecue instead of particular parts, I had so little confidence in the strength of my vision that I thought of calling the work *Memoirs* and treating the subject in a more desultory and superficial manner than belongs to a regular history. I did not go to work in a business-like style till I broke ground on the troubles of the Netherlands. Perhaps my critics may find this out."

Although, as usual, Prescott had very moderate views about his book, the public fully appreciated the quality of the work, and six months after publication of the first two volumes it was evident that *Philip the Second* was to find even more favour than its predecessors. The historian made this note about it: "A settlement made with my publishers here last week enables me to speak of the success of the work. In England it has been published in four separate editions; one of them from the rival house of Routledge. It has been twice reprinted in Germany, and a Spanish translation of it is now in course of publication at Madrid. In this country (the United States) eight thousand copies have been sold, while the sales of the preceding works have been so much improved by the impulse received from this that nearly thirty thousand volumes of them have been disposed of by my Boston publishers, from whom I have received seventeen thousand dollars for the *Philip* and the other works the last six months. So much for the lucre!"

The illustrious Scot, William Robertson, wrote a history of the reign of Charles V. In his day, however, information about the life of the Emperor after his abdication was lacking, since the archives of Simancas, containing the original correspondence of Charles V and his household, were closed to native as well as foreign scholars. Prescott had full access to the documents in what he terms the "dusty recesses" at Simancas, and from these manuscript sources was able to show conclusively that the monarch, instead of remaining dead to the world in the monastery to which he retired, took not merely an interest but a very active part in the management of affairs. In this way fresh light was shed on the character of Charles, and the events of the period were narrated by Prescott from a different and more accurate point of view than had previously been available. Prescott confined his work to the life of Charles V after his abdication.

Prescott held the view that the history of Philip II was the history of Europe during the latter half of the sixteenth century. During this period the doctrines of the Reformation were agitating the minds of men so violently that the very foundations of the Romish hierarchy were shaken in the fierce contest which divided Christendom. It happened that Philip, both from his personal character and from his position as sovereign of the most potent monarchy in Europe, was placed at the head of the party that strove to uphold the fortunes of the ancient Church.

The policy of Philip led him to interfere constantly in the internal affairs of the other European States, and hence Prescott found it necessary to look for the materials for his history quite as much outside the Peninsula as within it. Prescott was careful and thorough in preparing the groundwork for his study, taking the utmost pains to make a complete survey of the evidence relating to his chosen subject. He devoted himself with unwearied assiduity to the examination of the principal collections of documents both in England and on the Continent. The records examined included those at the British Museum and the State Paper Office in London, the Library of the Dukes of Burgundy in Brussels, the Archives of the Empire in Vienna, the Library of the University of Leyden, the Royal Library at The Hague, the then Royal Library of Paris, the Library of the Academy of History and the National Library at Madrid, and, above all, the papers in the ancient Archives of Simancas. In addition to public repositories, materials were drawn from the most notable private collections. Thus in Spain the historian had access to contemporary documents of the reign of Philip II in the family archives of the Marquis of Santa Cruz, whose illustrious ancestor first had charge of the Spanish Armada; the archives of Medina Sidonia, containing the papers of the duke who succeeded to the command of that ill-fated expedition; and the archives of the ducal house of Alva, a name associated with so many of the most memorable acts of the period. Prescott also turned repeatedly to the *Relazioni Venete*, the reports made by the ambassadors of Venice on their return from their foreign missions, which he described as, "those precious documents that contain so much instruction in respect to matters both of public and domestic interest".

Prescott had a sudden stroke of apoplexy in February 1858, but with his usual courage continued working, and was revising his *Mexico* when a second attack caused his death in January 1859. He gained wide and grateful recognition from a body of readers on both sides of the Atlantic. The *Conquest of Mexico* remains one of the most popular classics. It has been said that there is not a dull passage in all his histories, and this continues to be the view of many readers. His lasting favour rests largely on his vigorous and direct narrative. Because of his terrible affliction of half-blindness he had to see with the inward eye, and his genius enabled him to give to his pages the vivid colours of reality and life.

THE HISTORICAL WORKS OF PRESCOTT
WITH DATES OF PUBLICATION

1838   *The History of Ferdinand and Isabella.*
1843   *History of the Conquest of Mexico.*
1847   *The Conquest of Peru.*
1855-58   *History of Philip II.*
1856   *The Life of Charles V after his Abdication.*

LORD MACAULAY

from a photograph by Claudet

CHAPTER VIII

Lord Macaulay
(1800-1859)

THE family of Macaulay belonged originally to the Scottish highlands. The great-grandfather of the historian was the Rev. Aulay Macaulay, who was "greviously annoyed by a decreet obtained after the instance of the Laird of Ardchattan, taking away his stipend". Several of the descendants of this worthy entered the ministry.

The historian's grandfather, the Rev. John Macaulay, married Margaret, daughter of Colin Campbell, and was helped by the patronage of that powerful family. He became Presbyterian minister of the Kirk of Inveraray, in the headquarters of the Campbell country. His brother, the Rev. Kenneth Macaulay, was author of a history of St. Kilda. Thus Thomas Babington Macaulay, afterwards Lord Macaulay, who was born in 1800, inherited a tradition of both preaching and writing.

Origins leave their mark upon character and upon features. Carlyle, when on a visit to Lord Ashburton, happened to see Macaulay's face in repose, as he was turning over the pages of a book. "I noticed", he said, "the homely Norse features that you find everywhere in the Western Isles, and I thought to myself: 'Well! Anyone can see that you are an honest good sort of fellow, made out of oatmeal.'" As will be seen later, Macaulay took no such charitable view of Carlyle.

At boarding school he was marked by "his utter inability to play any sort of game", but he spent much time among books. His nephew remarks that early on, when writing home, "His letters began to smack of the library. His pen was over-charged with the metaphors and phrases of other men." As he grew older he was able to develop a facility in writing by having a good memory for what he read. His mind was not selective, but he could store away a mass of miscellaneous information. A great deal of this was quite useless, but some of it could be turned to account in his literary work.

The father's means were sufficient to enable him to send his son to Cambridge, and at the age of eighteen Macaulay went into residence at Trinity College. His nephew records that he revelled in the leisure and liberty which the university provided, with the power of passing at choice from the most perfect solitude to the most agreeable company. He was elected a Fellow of Trinity in 1824, and characteristically thought not of the opportunities for further study thus provided. Instead he noted with satisfaction that, "This gives me three hundred pounds a year, a stable for my horse, six dozen of audit ale every Xmas, a loaf and two pats of butter every morning, and a good dinner for nothing, with as many almonds and raisins as I can eat at dessert".

Then and afterwards Macaulay fully appreciated the good things of a material kind that the Colleges of Oxford and Cambridge had to offer. He never tired of recalling the days when, as an undergraduate, he supped at midnight on milk-punch and roast turkey. "I think", he said afterwards, "of the spacious and stately mansions of the heads of houses, of the commodious chambers of the fellows and scholars, of the refectories, the combination rooms, the bowling greens, the stabling, of the state and luxury of the great feast days, of the piles of old plate on the tables, of the savoury steam of the kitchens, of the multitude of geese and capons which turn at once on the spits, of the oceans of excellent ale in the butteries." Of things of the mind he says nothing. He omits any reference to the glory of the architecture of the Colleges; the great libraries and other facilities for research; or of any intellectual activities; his interests were elsewhere.

Soon after his election as a Fellow we find Macaulay beginning his profitable connection with journalism. Jeffrey, then the editor of the *Edinburgh Review,* was looking for new writers, and in January 1825, wrote to a friend in London, "Can you not lay your hands on some clever young man who would write for us? The original supporters of the work are getting old, and either too busy or too stupid, and here the young men are mostly Tories." Young Macaulay was a Whig, and was brought to the notice of Jeffrey. In August of the same year an article he had written on Milton was published in the *Journal,* being the first of many contributions. His whiggery was, however, strictly sedate and middle-class. "If they have the power", he wrote later of the people in a prophetic passage, "they will commit waste of every sort on the estate of mankind and transmit it to posterity impoverished and desolated."

Of the Milton article Professor F. C. Montague writes that, "Crude, garish, and superficial as this essay now seems to many readers, it then carried away the public". The literary element was grossly corrupted by political prejudice, but, "Its worst faults as a piece of criticism did not offend, for people were accustomed to criticism drugged with party politics". As other essays followed, for Macaulay could write freely, it became evident that a valuable recruit had been gained for the Whig party, then returning to favour after a lengthy exile in the political wilderness. Political leaders still had pocket boroughs in their gift, and upon the invitation of Lord Lansdowne the future historian was elected for one of these in 1830.

The chance of mixing more with the world, especially after entering Parliament, enabled Macaulay to shed some of his more obvious gaucherie, although in many ways his boorishness was too deep-seated ever to be eradicated. His sister Margaret kept a journal "with an artless candour", and notes on 24 March 1831, that, "Tom is very much improved in his appearance during the last two or three years. His figure is not so bad for a man of thirty as for a man of twenty-two. He dresses better, and his manners, from seeing a great deal of society, are very much improved."

Other forms of entertainment were available to the young politician, and of one reception at Lansdowne House he writes: "As to the company there was just everybody in London—the Chancellor, the First Lord of the Admiralty, Lord Mansfield, and a hideous Russian spy, whose face I see everywhere, with a star in his coat." For real enjoyment, however, dining-out retained its premier place, and this kind of hospitality was offered by Ministers to their supporters in the House. On 29 August 1831, Macaulay wrote to his sister Hannah: "I dined on Saturday with Lord Althorp, and yesterday with Sir James Graham. Both of them gave me exactly the same dinner. Turtle, turbot, venison, and grouse formed part of both entertainments." Russian spies may still be with us, but the glories of the dining-table have departed in this modern age of austerity.

Essay writing is a natural approach to the full-scale writing of history, and Macaulay gained his experience in this way. His essays frequently deal with historical personages, and his characteristic faults are very evident in them.   Thus it has been remarked about the one on *Warren Hastings* that it was written "with too little knowledge and too much assurance". Both Sir John Strachey and Sir James Stephen have exposed its grave inaccuracy.

Professor Montagu observes that, "A certain commonness in his thought could not but manifest itself in his style.   Macaulay is always the rhetorician, that is, he is always addressing a crowd, and he therefore instinctively omits what the average man will not instinctively appreciate.   Macaulay is, of all illustrious writers, the one least apt to be made an intimate, a lifelong companion by those who love literature.   Providence designed him to be the admiration of many, not the delight of a few."   Of his essays the historian Lord Acton wrote: "When you sit down to read Macaulay, remember that the Essays are really flashy and superficial.   He was not above par in literary criticism; his Indian articles will not hold water; and his two most famous reviews, on Bacon and Ranke, show his incompetence."

One of Macaulay's essays was on Goldsmith, and it is instructive to see how he approaches his subject.   It is almost incredible that anyone with any pretensions as a *littérateur* should fail to appreciate the genius of Goldsmith, but it certainly happens with Macaulay.   Goldsmith himself is treated with contemptuous condescension as a kind of half-witted buffoon, and his imperishable writings are lightly dismissed in a few entirely inadequate phrases as the fumbling efforts of a tyro whose work is beneath serious consideration.   The obtuse arrogance and blindness of Macaulay in this matter is quite inexcusable, as also his assumption of the right to pass judgment on one so infinitely his superior.

Macaulay was complacently confident about the merit of his history even before he began to compose it.   Thus he notes in his journal on 18 December 1838: "I stayed at home till late, reading and meditating.   I have thought a good deal during the last few days about my History.   The great difficulty of a work of this kind is the beginning.   After much consideration

I think that I can manage, by the help of an introductory chapter or two, to glide imperceptibly into the full current of my narrative. I really think that posterity will not willingly let my book die." And strangely he did manage to make many of his contemporaries take him at his own valuation.

He desired to excel as a popular writer. Towards the close of 1841 he wrote: "I have at last begun my historical labours. English history, from 1688 to the French Revolution, is even to educated people almost a *terra incognita*. I will venture to say that it is quite an even chance whether even such a man as Empson, or Senior, can repeat accurately the names of the Prime Ministers of that time in order. The materials for an amusing narrative are immense. I shall not be satisfied unless I produce something which shall for a few days supersede the last fashionable novel on the tables of young ladies."

Thus he deliberately set out to compete with the light novels of his day. Sir Charles Firth remarks with regard to this passage: "It would be unfair to take too literally the words of a casual letter to a friend, but it looks a little as if Macaulay made knowledge of history to consist in remembering a list of names, and the aim of history the production of an entertaining story."

In his later days Macaulay spent a holiday in Scotland. At Tarbet a young woman asked who he was, and upon being told that it was Macaulay who wrote the history, replied, "Oh! I thought it was considered only a romance!" An interesting and illuminating contemporary comment.

The historian's nephew expresses the opinion that one reason for his success lay in that, to extraordinary fluency and facility he united patient and persistent diligence. "As soon as he had got into his head all the information relating to any particular episode in his History, he would sit down and write off the whole story at a headlong pace; sketching in the outlines under the genial and audacious impulse of a first conception. As soon as Macaulay had finished his rough draft, he began to fill it in at the rate of six sides of foolscap every morning; written in so large a hand, and with such a multitude of erasures, that the whole six pages were, on an everage, compressed into two pages of print. This portion he called his task, and he was never quite easy unless he completed it daily."

When Macaulay published the first two volumes of his *History of England*, in 1848, copies sold extremely freely, and the outcome was very profitable both to the author and his publishers. As Montague notices, the volumes "were received with general though not unqualified praise by the critics, and with unequalled enthusiasm by the multitude of readers". The distinction between informed and uncritical opinion is important, and was to become more marked. Thus when two more volumes appeared in 1855 there was "a strong admixture of censure" in the reviews. This was inevitable, for "The great and real merits of the *History* were on the surface, and when the first volumes appeared had carried all before them. Since then the public had had leisure to re-read and to criticise, and in the new volumes the defects, also real and serious, attracted more attention."

J. S. Mill, a contemporary of the historian, wrote in his diary: "It would be unfair to measure the work of any age by that of its popular objects of literary or artistic admiration. Otherwise one might say that the present age will be known and estimated by posterity as the age which thought Macaulay a great writer." Lord Morley pointed out how Macaulay's style was copied in newspaper journalism, and the German critic Arminius coined a word "Macaulayese", so called, he says, "because it has the same internal and external characteristics as Macaulay's style; the external characteristic being a hard metallic movement with nothing of the soft play of life, and the internal characteristic being a perpetual semblance of hitting the right nail on the head without the reality". There is a record of a conversation between W. E. H. Lecky and Herbert Spencer: "We talked much about style in writing . . . about the bad writing of Addison, about the especial atrocity of Macaulay, whose style 'resembles low organisations, being a perpetual repetition of similar parts'."

Macaulay had not the temper and quality of mind of a great historian. As Sir Charles Firth says of his work: "The narrowness of view, the partiality, and the prejudice, which mar large portions of Macaulay's History, seriously diminish its permanent value as an account of a period of English history."

To Matthew Arnold the historian seemed like a giant embodiment of the English middle-class Philistine, smashing down all beauty in his path. It is not surprising, therefore, that Arthur Bryant should remark that, "At the time when Macaulay was working, English historical scholarship was at its lowest ebb". In other words there was a close relationship between his insensitiveness in the arts and his coarse-grained literary style. Without doubt, too, there was a connection between these and the moral insensibility which allowed him to suppress and manipulate facts about historical personages, and pervert the truth about political opponents.

As Macaulay was lacking in a sense of proportion he could not control the scale of his work. His pen had the more freedom because of the absence of serious historical research. His intention was to carry his history to the nineteenth century, but he succeeded only in dealing with a period of just over twenty-five years, the record of which sprawled over eight volumes.

There was probably never a historian who undertook so little research, and who wrote with so little knowledge. Lord Acton, while praising Macaulay's literary powers, remarks that, "He knew nothing respectably before the seventeenth century; he knew nothing of foreign history, of religion, philosophy, science or art. He is, I am persuaded, grossly, basely unfair."

While Acton rightly felt that Macaulay was under a serious handicap in failing to appreciate the extensive influence of religion on the course of history, it is evident from passages in his writings that his position in this matter was, at least in part, deliberately assumed, and that he had strong private views which it was not diplomatic to express in his history.

In his journal there are several references to ecclesiastical matters in connection with visits to the Continent. On one occasion he attended service in a Catholic church in Marseilles. "The buildings and its decorations were wretched", he wrote. "There was a daub of God the Father . . . a wooden doll without beauty as expressly representing the Virgin—and so forth. I staid to the end, wondering that so many reasonable beings could come together to see a man bow, drink, bow again, wipe a cup, wrap up a napkin, spread his arms and gesticulate with his hands, and to hear a low muttering which they could not understand interrupted by the occasional jangling of a bell.

The lowest field preaching is respectable compared with this mummery."

His practical outlook is revealed on such occasions as when he wrote: "Rome is a city of priests. Trade and agriculture seem only to be tolerated as subsidiary to devotion. Men are allowed to work because, unless somebody works, nobody can live; and, if nobody lives, nobody can pray." A good refutal of the claims of those who believe the importance of the "next world" to be paramount!

Macaulay had a zest for life which must have been of great assistance to him in maintaining his high output of literary work. He enjoyed, for example, visiting localities where events had taken place that were deserted in his *History,* and his narrative gained in freshness from the trouble he took in this way. A case in point when he stayed for some weeks at the village inn of Zoyland in Somerset, a place celebrated as being the scene of the Duke of Monmouth's defeat at the battle of Sedgemoor. From another point of view it was no hardship to visit rural Somerset at a favourable time of the year; and the freedom from distractions there no doubt enabled him to write freely and at speed.

It could hardly be taken as a sign of greatness that Macaulay's works sold well. His writings were easy to understand, and this may account for the popularity they enjoyed for many years in schools. Of his style Saintsbury says: "Suggestion it has none: it cannot, in the subtle way which the greater styles use, supply keys to unlock and power to set working, in the reader's mind, chambers of machinery supplemental to the author's own. But what Macaulay meant the reader understands at once and to the very full. And the general public, which was mainly in tune with him answered by buying Macaulay as no historian had been bought before." Another reason for the good sales was probably the prosperity of the Victorian era, and the pride in our history which resulted from growing wealth and power.

It was no mere whim or misconception which led to Macaulay's *History* being accorded such a high place in popular esteem. It is probably not even sufficient to give full weight to such undoubtedly important factors as his journalistic skill; the way that he gratified national self-esteem; or his good fortune in writing when the numbers of the reading public had recently been greatly increased. In such cases there is usually some more fundamental element, some way in which a writer is in intimate accord with his period, and is expressing some sentiment or belief about which there is pent-up feeling seeking an outlet. The Whig bias which Macaulay showed in such uncompromising fashion may well have counted for a great deal in establishing his reputation. Ranke suggests that the Revolution of 1688, which Macaulay takes as his starting point, was of particular consequence because it marked the turning point in the contest between absolute monarchy, and monarchy limited by a parliamentary constitution. As the principle of a mixed constitution came to be widely adopted, the English model was copied by other nations. "This general tendency", says Ranke,* "is one cause of the immense success which Macaulay's *History*, appearing just at the right moment, had in Europe. Up to that time the Tory view, as represented by Hume, had not yet been driven from the field. Macaulay decided the victory of the Whig view."

As well as being very proud of his remarkable powers of memory, Macaulay had implicit faith in them. This was unwise, for human frailty is apt to be most evident among the unwary. From his miscellaneous and unsystematic early reading he formed a collection of mental impressions or images which to him were extremely real and vivid. With their aid he constructed theories about persons and events which he afterwards failed to differentiate from external fact. "My accuracy as to facts", he wrote, "I owe to a cause which many men would not confess. It is due to my love of castle-building. The past is in my mind soon constructed into a romance." He was led in this way into a quicksand of error. Thus in presenting the two great protagonists James II and William of Orange, he began with a closed mind, having established fabulous conceptions without any proper examination of the available evidence. This uncritical attitude arose directly from his self-confident reliance on his recollections of very desultory reading. He was taken off his guard partly through lack of that humility of spirit which has so often been an attribute of the truly great, and in part through lack of appreciation of the need for that quiet studious research which, if he had undertaken it, would

* *History of England*, by Leopold von Ranke, 1875, Book 6, p. 29.

doubtless have meant the sacrifice of the wealth and worldly success that became his.

A serious defect in Macaulay's *History,* and one which pervades the whole work, is the habit of dogmatic assertion. Points which are very doubtful or debatable are declared without reservation as positive truths. Firth says in this connection that "Macaulay's dogmatism implies a kind of blindness, a mistaken conviction that the whole of the necessary evidence was before him". This was a dangerous weakness for a historian, especially one so ill-equipped, but was fully in keeping with Macaulay's character. We are reminded that Lord Melbourne is reputed to have said that he wished he could be, "as cocksure about anything as Macaulay is about everything". Unfortunately the uncritical often accept as virtues the most blatant faults of demagoguery.

Partly because of political bias Macaulay misjudges Marlborough, and rejects the simple and natural interpretation of the facts to indulge motives which he himself imagines. "It is unusual", says Firth, "for a historian of sober and well-balanced judgment to claim such omniscience about men's motives". When this error is repeated, Firth continues: "Here again omniscience intervenes to supply the want of evidence. Macaulay has formed beforehand a clear conception of Marlborough's character; he is therefore absolutely convinced that he knows motives, though there is no record which reveals them, and suppresses facts and evidence which tell against his theory." It is for reasons such as these that, as Professor Legouis observes, "Macaulay is disparaged by fastidious minds".

Croce holds that German and French historians have often been partisan. By contrast British historians have felt the need for defence or offence in such matters much less, because of the long tradition of political liberty which our country has enjoyed. But although in general we have been able to contemplate history more serenely, various party tendencies have been displayed in the histories of Macaulay, Grote, Carlyle and others. Macaulay combined the writing of his *History* with his duties as Minister of War, and it is significant that, as a member of a Whig Cabinet, he should plan his *History* to cover the period in which he believed he could display the progressive triumphs of Whiggery. "No man", says Cotter Morison, "was ever less of a philosopher or more of a politician than Macaulay. He had an eye to business, not to abstract truth."

It is an amiable characteristic of Macaulay that, living in an age of rapid progress and great security, he should be proud of our national achievements. "In consequence partly of our geographical and partly of our moral position", he says, "we have, during several generations, been exempt from evils which have elsewhere impeded the efforts and destroyed the fruits of industry." It may be doubted how far this is true today, or whether we can still claim that, "Every man has felt entire confidence that the State would protect him in the possession of what has been earned by his diligence and hoarded by his self-denial". In another passage he writes, "Science has flourished and has been applied to practical purposes on a scale never before known. The consequence is that a change to which the history of the old world furnishes no parallel has taken place in our country."

It was comforting for the town-dweller to read a passage like the following, even if there was risk of undue complacency being bred. "The street which now affords to the artisan, during the whole night, a secure, a convenient and a brilliantly lighted walk was, a hundred and sixty years ago, so dark after sunset that he would not have been able to see his hand, so ill paved that he would have run constant risk of breaking his neck, and so ill watched that he would have been in imminent danger of being knocked down and plundered of his small earnings." There is evident here a clear perception of the kind of benefit resulting from the industrial revolution, and of the social progress which we have since continued to enjoy in ever increasing measure. The views expressed were understood and appreciated by many in the Victorian era, itself so rich in practical achievement: Macaulay was truly a child of his age.

From the point of view of both inclination and equipment it was natural for Macaulay to regard history as what he termed "a department of literature". In the past generation there has been a swing to the other extreme, with historians tending to regard history as a branch of science. The modern habit has been to devote much painstaking attention to the accumulating of detailed information, but to present this in an amorphous form, without even a sense of proportion in distinguishing between facts of major significance and those of no conceivable interest or importance. Macaulay, on the other hand, was much concerned with presenting his material pleasantly, but failed badly on the scientific side.

Another authority, Dr. William Wallace, while finding some features about the historian deserving of praise, says that, "The reputation of Macaulay is certainly not what it was during his lifetime or immediately after his death. He has been convicted of historical inaccuracy, of sacrificing truth for the sake of epigram, of allowing personal dislike and party bias to distort his views of men and incidents. As a thinker he is deficient in balance, repose, inwardness, and modesty. He not infrequently confounds the foaming hurry of his own words with the march of events; his style sometimes degenerates into garishness; occasionally when he plays the censor, he almost sinks into insolent brutality."

It is constantly evident that Macaulay wrote as he spoke; the historian is merged into a political orator. Unfortunately the technique of the written and spoken word are very different. For the orator it is often necessary to repeat himself by explaining his point in different ways, so as to drive home his argument and make sure that it is understood by the most inattentive or least intelligent of his audience. To achieve his aim, and to reach as large a proportion of his listeners as possible, he must over-emphasize, for, as Taine puts it,* "Il faut qu'ils comprennent trop pour comprendre assey". The writer of history, on the other hand, normally only states his case once, for his readers can always refer back to any passage which they may wish to study with extra care.

The exuberance of Macaulay, and the other limitations from which he suffered, led him to indulge in serious verbal excess. In contrast to Gibbon, who wrote for the scholar, he would use a whole sentence to do the work of a single adjective. He habitually chose, too, the pretentious phrase in preference to the plainer and more natural one. Yet he was far from clumsy in his faults. He deliberately catered for a numerous lower middle-class public who were then newly literate, and had not acquired any critical standards. To such readers the devices he employed to excite and keep their attention were thoroughly acceptable.

*Histoire de la litterature anglaise, Vol. V, by Hippolyte-Adolphe Taine.

In an acute piece of observation Bagehot suggests that Macaulay was remarkable for his insensibility. After attaining considerable power in his earlier years he ceased to develop. His views remained rigid, and his mind seemed unable to enrich itself by experience. It was characteristic of him that he maintained that dead authors were more fascinating than living people. He had a mind "impassive to our daily life, to joys and sorrows, incapable of the deepest sympathies, a prey to print. The mass of men have stronger ties and warmer hopes. The exclusive devotion to books tires. We require to love and hate, to act and live." In consequence of his temperament he was incapable of understanding or appreciating men of genius whose minds were finer and more sensitive than his own.

To a man of so cold a nature the vivid Tudor and Stuart periods of our history could have little appeal, and his handling of them was defective. Passionate feeling was so foreign to him that when he met it either in Cavalier or Puritan, and both represented an extreme, he judged it with chill aloofness. It has been said that he wrote too much as though the whole history of England was a preface to the Act of Catholic Emancipation and the first Reform Act.

Macaulay had no confidence in democracies. In a letter to an American friend he says, "I have long been convinced that institutions purely democratic must, sooner or later, destroy liberty or civilisation, or both. In Europe, where the population is dense, the effect of such institutions would be almost instantaneous. What happened lately in France is an example. In 1848 a pure democracy was established there. During a short time there was reason to expect a general spoliation, a national bankruptcy, a new partition of the soil, a maximum of prices, a ruinous load of taxation laid on the rich for the purpose of supporting the poor in idleness. Such a system would, in twenty years, have made France as poor and barbarous as the France of the Carlovingians. Happily, the danger was averted; and now there is a despotism, a silent tribune, an enslaved press. Liberty is gone, but civilisation has been saved."

He continues, "I have not the smallest doubt that if we had a purely democratic Government here the effect would be the same. Either the poor would plunder the rich, and civilization would perish; or order and prosperity would be saved by a strong military government and liberty would perish. You may think that your country enjoys an exemption from these evils. I will frankly own to you that I am of a very different opinion. . . . The time will come when New England will be as thickly populated as Old England. You will have your Manchesters and your Birminghams, and in them hundreds of thousands of artisans will assuredly be sometimes out of work. Then your institutions will be fairly brought to the test. Distress everywhere makes the labourer mutinous and discontented, and inclines him to listen with eagerness to agitators. It is quite plain that your Government will never be able to restrain a distressed and discontented majority. For with you the majority is the Government, and has the rich, who are always a minority, absolutely at its mercy."

It was perhaps natural for Macaulay, always lacking in imaginative powers, to think of the New World merely as a place where the worst conditions of Europe would be duplicated. He had no conception of the wonderful developments that were to take place in the United States, giving a freer and fuller life to the common citizen than anything known before.

There can be no doubt that Macaulay was a man of very curious limitations. Yet while, for instance, he could cultivate the study of classical authors for reasons of social prestige, he was capable of making comments which showed shrewd observation, as when he said that, "Most people read all the Greek that they ever read before they are five and twenty. They never find time for such studies afterwards till they are in the decline of life; and then their knowledge of the language is in a great measure lost, and cannot easily be recovered. Accordingly, almost all the ideas that people have of Greek literature, are ideas formed while they were still very young."

It is striking how arrogant Macaulay was in his literary judgments, as when he described Wordsworth as "a humbug, a bore and a rat". Dickens's style he declared to be vulgar. He could not be persuaded that Carlyle ever wrote a sentence that was not meaningless gibberish. "Carlyle is here undergoing a water cure", he wrote on one occasion from Clifton, "I have not seen him yet. But his water-doctor said the other day, 'You wonder at his eccentric opinions and style. It is all stomach.

I shall set him to rights. He will go away quite a different person.' If he goes away writing commonsense and good English, I shall declare myself a convert to hydropathy."

In an interesting summary of the historian's characteristics, Professor Saintsbury declares that he was a hater of abstract principles and extremely narrow in thought; contemptuous of all things and periods, such as the Middle Ages and even the Renaissance, which he had not taken the trouble to understand; sure that all things worth understanding could be understood easily; compensating his liberalism in politics by a rather obstinate conservatism in style and philosophy; exposed to the charge of shallowness, and limited in almost every direction; healthy but imperfectly developed. There was, in fact, an entire absence of the warm sympathy and breadth of vision necessary for interpreting the past.

The popularity of Macaulay's *History* brought him some recognition. In June 1853, for example, he became a Doctor of Civil Law at Oxford. The undergraduates did not give him an altogether favourable reception. He notes in his journal that, "When I entered someone called out 'History of England!' Then came a great tumult of applause and hissing; but the applause greatly predominated." The Prince Consort also offered him the Chair of Modern History at Cambridge, but he did not accept.

The commercial success of the history was outstanding. In February 1856, there is an entry in his journal to the effect that, "Longman called. It is necessary to reprint. This is wonderful. 26,500 copies sold in ten weeks: I should not wonder if I made £20,000 clear this year by literature." In March 1856, Longman's did in fact pay him a cheque for the then great sum of £20,000. "What a sum to be gained by one edition of a book!" as Macaulay truly remarked.

The historian consulted Henry Thornton, a partner in Williams Deacon's Bank, about investments. The distinction was explained to him at some length between the different classes of Spanish Stock—Active, Passive and Deferred. "I think", said Macaulay, "that I catch your meaning. Active Spanish Bonds profess to pay interest now, and do not. Deferred Spanish Bonds profess to pay interest at some future time, and will not. Passive Spanish Bonds profess to pay interest neither

I

now, nor at any future time." It is hardly necessary to add
that he did not invest in Spanish bonds.

The substantial fortune which Macaulay accumulated enabled him to live in good style and to entertain. In a pleasant
letter to his neice Margaret he writes: "Michaelmas will, I hope,
find us all at Clapham over a noble goose. Do you remember
the beautiful Puseyite hymn on Michaelmas day? It begins:

> Though Quakers scowl, though Baptists howl,
> Though Plymouth Brethren rage,
> We Churchmen gay will wallow today
> In apple sauce, onions and sage.

> Ply knife and fork, and draw the cork,
> And have the bottle handy:
> For each slice of goose will introduce
> A thimbleful of brandy."

He knew well how to provide the pleasure of the table for
young relatives, and kept a youthful zest for that kind of
entertainment. On another occasion he wrote in his journal:
"Fanny brought George and Margaret, with Charley Cropper,
to the Albany at one yesterday. I gave them some dinner; fowl,
ham, marrow-bones, tart, ice, olives and champagne."

Macaulay was raised to the peerage in August 1857 and in
the following month wrote: "I have at odd moments been
studying the Peerage. I ought to be better informed about the
assembly in which I am to sit." Very soon he could recite the
entire roll of the House of Lords. And a few days later another
entry in his diary read, "More exercise for my memory—Second
titles". Then he returned to his old loves, the Oxford and
Cambridge Calendars: "I have now", he said, "the whole of
our University Fasti by heart." There was, in fact, no limit to
this extraordinary habit of learning by heart long lists of persons
and things—how accurately probably no one was able to say.

The historian did not live long to enjoy his honours. He
continued in spite of increasing ill-health to work until the end
upon "his vast but unfinished history". His death took place
in London on 28 December 1859. That evening he complained
to his butler that he felt tired. His man suggested that it would
be restful for him to lie on the sofa. He rose as if to move, sat
down again, and ceased to breathe. Thus he died quite peacefully and without pain.

THE HISTORICAL WORKS OF MACAULAY
WITH DATES OF PUBLICATION

1841-44 *Critical and Miscellaneous Essays.*

1848 *The History of England from the accession of James II,* Vols. I and II.

1856 *The History of England from the accession of James II,* Vols. III and IV.

1861 *The History of England from the accession of James II,* Vol. V. (The work was unfinished at the time of the historian's death.)

CHAPTER IX

James Anthony Froude
(1818-1894)

IT is usually instructive to consider the immediate forebears
of any man who achieves marked distinction, for heredity
plays an important part. The influence of ancestry can be
traced very clearly in the case of Froude. His is an example of
the striking personality which is apt to emerge when two widely
different strains are united. The simpler elements which his
parents represented formed in him a complex genius which,
while the ingredients were clearly recognizable, was unlike anything that had gone before.

The Froudes were Devon men. The historian's father was
Archdeacon of Totnes, and besides being a dignitary of the
Church was prominent in county affairs. He was a landowner
with a rent-roll of nearly three thousand a year, and in addition
to his clerical duties was active in the management of his extensive estates. And his boundless energy had to find still further
outlets, so that we find him interested in politics as a zealous
Tory, and a magistrate attentive to his duties in dealing with
poachers and the like. A strong man, too, must have exercise,
and the Archdeacon was a hard rider to the hounds, esteemed as
a good judge of horse-flesh, and usually the best mounted man
in the field. He was a typical representative of the paternal
stock, and it will be observed that intellectual interests were not
prominent.

On the maternal side there was a remarkable contrast. The
Archdeacon married Margaret Spedding, the daughter of an
old college friend. She was a woman of great beauty, and trans-
mitted her good looks to her famous son. More important,
however, is the fact that the Speddings, though not robust in
physique, had mental attributes of a high order. They had
earned some reputation in both letters and science. Thus in
the literary ability of Froude we can no doubt trace a quality
inherited from his mother's family; but in his taste for an open-
air life, and in his admiration for the Elizabethans and our

JAMES ANTHONY FROUDE
from a photograph by Elliott & Fry

pioneers of Empire, we can see traits that came from his father's line.

James Anthony Froude was born in Devon on St. George's Day, 23 April 1818, which was also the anniversary of the birth of Shakespeare. This was to prove specially appropriate because of the splendid patriotism which became one of his most characteristic merits. His childhood was not altogether happy, as his mother died when he was young and as for some time he himself was delicate. He was sent to Westminster at the age of eleven, but suffered from the unsatisfactory conditions which then prevailed there. There was gross bullying, and Herbert Paul records that Froude, who at that time was incapacitated by hernia, was wakened in the dormitory by the hot points of cigars burning holes in his face, made drunk by being forced to swallow brandy punch, and repeatedly thrashed. After bad nights other miseries followed in the daytime. He was more than half starved, for the bigger boys had the pick of the joints at dinner, leaving little but the bone for the younger ones. At this period much the same state of affairs ruled at Winchester and Eton.

When Froude had been at Westminster for four years it was abundantly clear that he was gaining little here. Although a brilliant boy when he entered the school, he had been too ill-treated and under-fed to make proper progress, for the mind could not function well when physical conditions were so bad. At fifteen, therefore, he was brought home, and left much to his own devices. He spent most of his days in the open air. His health improved rapidly as he lived an active life by the river, in the woods, or on the moors of the beautiful Devon country. In the evenings an excellent library enabled him to keep up his studies, so that he grew strong both in mind and body.

From this time he never lost his taste for an open-air life, and it is evident from a description which his son* gave of him in latter years that he fully maintained the athletic tradition of the Froudes. He grew to be a powerful and active man of nearly six feet. He liked old clothes, but they were made by a good London tailor. As became a Devon man he loved the water, was passionately fond of yachting, and was at home in any kind of boat, from a racing eight to a trawler. His intrepid spirit caused him when sailing to take risks with his life and his gear. In

*Commander Ashley Anthony Froude, C.M.G., O.B.E., B.A,. D.L., J.P.

addition he was a good shot and an expert fisherman who made his own flies.

In 1836 Froude went up to Oxford, and matriculated at Oriel. The first two years of his residence were not very fruitful, for a good allowance brought many pleasures within his scope, and the ambition to excel in intellectual pursuits had not developed. This is not to suggest that he was lacking in strength of character, for the reverse was the case. He had already developed interests, for example, which were to influence his future work. Thus his affection for the sea was directly linked with his knowledge of those "forgotten worthies", the old sea-dogs of Devon, whose exploits he was to recount in such spirited fashion. And a mind of the calibre of Froude's could not lie dormant for long, so that in his third year a great change in his outlook took place. As he himself said long afterwards: "The consciousness of duty, whatever its origin, is to the moral nature of man what life is to the seed-cells of all organised creatures: the condition of its coherence, the elementary force in virtue of which it grows." He took his degree in 1840.

After graduation Froude was for a time tutor to the son of the Rev. Mr. Cleaver, a "dignified, stately clergyman of the Evangelical school", who was rector of Delgany in County Wicklow. In this way he early had first-hand acquaintance with the Irish, about whom he was afterwards to write: "Two things I saw clearly. One was the strength and beauty of the religious faith by which the Cleavers and their friends lived. The other was the misery, squalor, and chronic discontent of the Catholic population." Before returning to England he made a tour through the south of Ireland, "where I saw superstition and irreverence, solid churches, well-fed priests, and a starving peasantry in rags".

When Froude returned to Oxford in 1842 he won the Chancellor's Prize for an English essay on the influence of political economy in the development of nations. In that year, too, he was elected to a Devonshire Fellowship at Exeter, a condition of which was that he should take orders.

Newman, one of the leaders of the Oxford Movement, was at this time seeking a means of refuting the ideas expressed by two of the great historians. Hume had argued against the probability of miracles, and Gibbon had enquired when miracles had ceased. Newman believed, in common with many Roman Catholics, that miracles had never ceased. He thought that, if the truth of miracles could be proved, this would demonstrate to the people that supernatural power resided in the Church. He therefore planned a series of tracts on the lives of the saints, and asked Froude to help him, being entirely sanguine about the result. It was a mistake, however, to chose so intelligent and honest an assistant, for Froude had complete intellectual integrity. No evidence could be found of investigation into facts. It soon became clear to Froude that the Church accepted without question tales of the wildest and most foolish kind, and regarded even the most crazy imaginings as solemn proof of the miraculous. He says: "St. Patrick I found once lighted a fire with icicles, changed a French marauder into a wolf, and floated to Ireland on an altar stone. I thought it nonsense. I found it eventually uncertain whether Patricius was not a title, and whether any single apostle of that name had so much as existed." Further research in hagiology bred more scepticism in the historian. It seemed to him that a religion based on such stories of the saints as those he met with was a religion nurtured in lies. He accordingly took the only course open to him and broke off his connection with Newman.

In 1844 the *Vestiges of Creation* appeared, the famous work in which Robert Chambers anticipated some of the doctrines of Darwin; dispensed with the need for the special creation of each plant and animal; and demonstrated that natural phenomena were due to natural causes. A lively impression was made on Froude when he read the book.

Froude's outlook gradually matured, and in 1847 he published his *Shadows of the Clouds* under a pseudonym, followed by his *Nemesis of Faith* in 1848. Of the latter work, written with startling power, it has been said that in it, "the solemnity and sadness of religious scepticism are relieved by a singularly tender and earnest humanity". Professor Hume Brown remarks that these two books taken together, "prove that Froude had lost his faith in the fundamental doctrines of the Christian religion". The future historian had in truth reached full maturity with unexpected suddenness. He saw clearly the sacrifices that would be demanded of him, but showed the greatness of his mind by going forward with courage. Of his *Nemesis* he said: "There is something in the thing, I know; for I cut a hole in my heart, and wrote with the blood." These are not extravagant words, for he found it exceedingly painful to break away from his early beliefs, to offend his father, and to discard the clerical traditions of his family. The consequences, too, as he had anticipated, were extremely serious for him. The Senior Tutor at Exeter, the College of which he was a Fellow, burnt a copy of the book in public during a lecture in the College Hall. The Rector and Fellows demanded that he should resign his Fellowship, on the grounds that the book was heretical. Although his legal position was secure, and expulsion would not have been possible, Froude was much too proud and sensitive to remain, and resigned at once. By doing so he sacrificed a career for the sake of his principles. If he had adopted the prudent course of holding fast the storm would probably have blown over after a time, but as it was he forsook an assured and comfortable living for one which was quite uncertain. He found himself suddenly in the precarious position of having to earn a living by his pen, while even his father refused to have anything to do with him; the Archdeacon, hoping the short commons might cure free thought, stopped his allowance. Unbelief was a serious matter in those days, particularly for the son of an Archdeacon.

Froude remained critical of the classics and the clergy. A generation after he left Oxford he wrote: "What I deplore in our present higher education is the devotion of so much effort and so many precious years to subjects which have no practical bearing upon life. We had a theory at Oxford that our system, however defective in many ways, yet developed in us some especially precious human qualities. Classics and philosophy are called there *literae humaniores*. They are supposed to have an effect on character, and to be specially adapted for creating ministers of religion. The training of clergymen is, if anything, the special object of Oxford teaching. . . . We have had thirty years of unexampled clerical activity among us; while by the side of it there has sprung up an equally astonishing development of moral dishonesty. Many a hundred sermons have I heard in England, but never one that I can recollect on common honesty."

A little later he continues with this passage: "Classical philosophy, classical history and literature, taking, as they do, no hold upon the living hearts and imagination of men in this modern age, leave their working intelligence a prey to wild imaginations, and make them incapable of really understanding the world in which they live. If the clergy knew as much of the history of England and Scotland as they know about Greece and Rome, and if they had been ever taught to open their eyes and see what is actually round them instead of groping among books to find what men did or thought at Alexandria or Constantinople fifteen hundred years ago, they would grapple more effectively with the moral pestilence which is poisoning all the air."

His strong practical bias caused him to make this biting condemnation of the Oxford of his mature years; "A young man going to Oxford learns the same things which were taught there two centuries ago; but, unlike the old scholars, he learns no lessons of poverty along with it. In his three years course he will have tasted luxuries unknown to him at home, and contracted habits of self-indulgence which make subsequent hardships unbearable: while his antiquated knowledge, such as it is, has fallen out of the market; there is no demand for him; he is not sustained by the respect of the world, which finds him ignorant of everything in which it is interested. He is called educated; yet, if circumstances throw him on his own resources, he cannot earn a sixpence for himself. An Oxford education fits a man extremely well for the trade of a gentleman. I do not know for what other trade it does fit him as at present constituted."

It is remarkable how little conditions have changed at Oxford since Froude's day. Thus Barry* wrote in 1939: "Nobody can understand Oxford unless he remembers that the University was created by a religious tradition. Religion is still taken for granted in a way which would not be possible or conceivable in universities of more recent foundation, and exercises a potent influence, not less strong because undefinable, on university teaching and life. There is probably no place in the world where such lavish provision is made both officially and unofficially for the teaching and practice of religion."

To support himself after leaving Oxford Froude became for a time private tutor to the family of Mr. Darbyshire, a rich

* Rev. F. R. Barry in *Oxford University Handbook*, 1939, pp. 277-278.

manufacturer of Manchester, who would have taken him into his own firm if the attractions of literature had not soon become too strong. Authorship was a natural resource for Froude, and he brought to his task a vivid personality, keen intelligence, unwearied industry and brilliant powers of writing. In spite of these advantages he had for a time a stiff struggle to make his way.

While on a visit to Charles Kingsley he met Mrs. Kingsley's sister, Charlotte Grenfell, who shortly afterwards became his wife. After his marriage Froude returned to his work in Manchester for a short time, but his bride did not like the northern city and a search was made for a country home. This was found in a beautiful spot in the Welsh hills, between Capel Curig and Beddgelert. The house stood on rising ground over-looking Dinas Lake, and was flanked by woods. Here the couple began a new life of unclouded happiness.

In June 1851, Froude wrote to Max Müller, the great philo-logist: "I shall be so glad to see you in July. Come and stay as long as work will let you, and you can endure our hospitality. We are poor, and so are not living at a high rate. I can't give you any wine, because I haven't a drop in the house, and you must bring your own cigars, as I am down to pipes. But, to set against that, you shall have the best dinner in Wales every day—fresh trout, Welsh mutton, as much bitter ale as you can drink; a bedroom and a little sitting-room joining it all for your own self, and the most beautiful look-out from the window that I have ever seen." It is not surprising that, with such attractions to offer, the Froudes found plenty of friends who were eager to come and visit them. The chief source of income during this period was from reviewing. Froude's writings were in such incomparable style that his pen was soon in constant demand.

The first historical writings which Froude undertook were in the form of essays, dealing especially with events in the age of Elizabeth. His splendidly inspired account of *England's Forgotten Worthies*, published in the *Westminster Review* in 1852, showed the eloquent powers that were to remain so evident in his work. In it he gave the truth with unflinching fidelity, as when he describes how four hundred Huguenots were flayed alive by the Spaniards, who invaded their settlement in Florida in spite of their respective countries being then at peace. As the crime was in the name of religion an inscription was placed over the bodies which read, "not as Frenchmen, but as heretics" A French privateer was able to take revenge on the pious but guilty villains, over whose remains he left the appropriate warning: "Not as Spaniards but as murderers." In contrast to the cruelties which the Spaniards perpetrated for their religion Froude shows the English navigators like Drake, Grenville, Hawkins and Raleigh as pioneers of civil and religious freedom.

From his writings for the *Reviews* his interest in history deepened, and Froude found it increasingly necessary to spend a good deal of his time in London in order to consult original documents. Thus through Sir Francis Palgrave, then Deputy Keeper of the Records, he obtained authority to examine the unpublished documents in the Chapter House at Westminster relating to the years towards the end of Wolsey's period of power and to the policy of Parliament after the Cardinal's fall.

In order that he might conduct his historical studies more intensively he moved his home back to his native county, having a house first at Babbicombe and later at Bideford. In this way he placed himself in the position of having much easier access to the capital through direct rail connections. Research work made heavy demands upon him. For the time being he had to give up his favourite pastimes of shooting and fishing, keeping himself fit, while in town, by joining an archery club.

It was inevitable that in this preparatory period the long hours spent in historical research should leave him with little time for the literary work by which he had been gaining a livelihood. This might have been a serious obstacle, but he was aided by the generosity of his publisher, John Parker, who had complete confidence in him and gave him necessary backing while he brought his enterprise to fruition.

The first two volumes of Froude's *History of England from the Fall of Cardinal Wolsey to the Spanish Armada* were published in 1856. The whole work was to prove, in his own words, "the companion of twenty years of pleasant but unintermittent labour", being completed in 1869. It was planned on a large scale, and finally occupied twelve volumes. It is difficult to conceive how laborious was the task that he set himself. No source of information was neglected, from the English documents at the British Museum, the Record Office and Hatfield, to the Spanish ones in the archives of Simancas. Herbert Paul remarks that nine-tenths of his authorities were in manuscript. They were in five languages, filling nine hundred volumes. And as Froude had no secretary he had to act as his own copyist.

It is remarkable that he was able to preserve his ardour and enthusiasm in spite of the constant toil he faced. The high quality of his work is in itself an indication that here was no mere compiler of records, but a historian of rare gifts. "Froude is a man of genius", said Jowett, and others were equally impressed. It was well said that he "expressed himself with the natural eloquence of a fastidious scholar", and that though the consummate dexterity of his style was only observed by trained critics, its ease and grace were the unconscious delight of the humblest reader.

Because Froude found history an attractive study he was able to make it interesting to others. The impression made even by one of his minor essays is described in these words by Bret Harte, the American. "The other night", wrote Harte, "I took up Longman's Magazine and began lazily to read something about the Spanish Armada. In the article I was reading the style caught me first; I became tremendously interested. Then I went through it breathlessly to the last word, which came all too soon. Now I am eager for the next instalment as I was when a boy for the next chapter of my Dickens or Thackeray. Don't laugh over my enthusiasm, but remember that I represent a considerable amount of average human nature, and that's what we all write for." One critic said that Froude wrote as much for the man of the world as for the student, and that "he was master of a style which by its rapidity, clearness and idiomatic grace is unsurpassed for the purposes of pure narrative". So it came about that he took a large share in bringing into existence a taste for history, so that today, for example, history in its different branches is one of the most popular subjects for study at the universities.

Professor Saintsbury expressed the view that Froude was an almost infinitely greater writer than his contemporaries Carlyle and Freeman. It was probably inevitable that there should be clashes between Freeman, a dull, conventional and strictly orthodox man, and Froude, who was so much his direct antithesis. In fact Froude's *History* was bitterly attacked by Freeman and his disciples. Freeman, being in an official position through holding the Chair of History at Oxford, was able to play the pundit, and sought to damage his victim by *ex cathedra* maledictions. Such, however, was the outstanding merit of Froude's work, from its scholarly style and its burning patriotism to its brilliant interpretation of historic scenes, that he gained a great reputation in the face of all obstacles.

It is significant that Froude is regarded in the United States as England's national historian. For the same underlying reasons he is hardly known on the Continent, having never been translated. This is no reproach to him, for while he had a warm admiration for the greatness of England he also saw her faults clearly. That he should not be appreciated abroad is, however, in part the consequence of his steadfast determination to do justice in his literary work to the glorious record of the English. Being ardently inspired by the rich achievements of the nation, he showed himself her eloquent champion. In a lesser man there might have been danger in this pre-occupation, but all that Froude wrote bore the hallmark of discrimination and good taste.

In his historical writing we can trace certain bold general conceptions which helped Froude to interpret the main events of the periods with which he was dealing. He attached great importance, for example, to the Reformation, which he considered was not merely a clash between rival dogmas, but a revolt of the laity against the clergy. It seemed to him that on the Continent as well as in England the reformers were, "fighting for truth, honesty, and private judgement against priestcraft and ecclesiastical tyranny". He himself stood for freedom of conscience, and held that the Church should be subordinate to the State.

Until Froude's day there had been persistent misrepresentation of both the character and policy of Henry VIII. The historian did valuable service in painting a much clearer picture of that monarch than had been available before. He showed that Henry, by repudiating the Papal authority, spoke for the English people, and brought substantial benefits to his country. In addition to showing Henry as a true patriot and a statesman of outstanding ability, he vindicates the private character of the King, and shows that the marriage with Anne Boleyn was not merely a matter of passion, but resulted largely from a patriotic wish to give the nation a male heir to the throne, with the settled conditions that a direct line of succession would maintain. If that had come about there would have been no Stuart dynasty and hence no Civil War.

It is noticeable that Froude has a keen sense of the dramatic, which implies also a sense of proportion. Macaulay, carried away by his own verbosity, allowed his history to get out of hand, so that he only completed part of the vague scheme with which he began. Froude, on the other hand, though also working on a major scale, kept close control of his plans. He chose deliberately to end with Elizabethan England at the height of her success, mistress of the seas, and with Spain vanquished. The problems with which he had been dealing had been worked out. The Reformation had been shown as an accomplished fact, with divine service being performed in English, and the English bible open for all that could read. The story had been magnificently told, and what remained of the great events which the historian had been considering was only the working out of the final details. Froude expresses the position by saying that "Chess-players, when they have brought their game to a point at which the result can be foreseen with certainty, regard their contest as ended, and sweep the pieces from the board".

Froude was distinguished as a man of letters as well as a historian. From early papers in the *Westminster Review* he proceeded to others in *Fraser's Magazine,* of which he was editor from 1860 to 1874. What he wrote in this way was collected in four volumes, and given the title of *Short Studies on Great Subjects.* While all these essays were elegant and full of interest, they varied in form from important studies of appropriate length to pleasant trifles like the fables or the Cat's pilgrimage. Froude built up an enviable reputation for *Fraser's.* He secured many notable contributors, some of whom were relatives or intimates of his own. He was acknowledged, too, to be an excellent editor; alert, appreciative, and discriminating.

It was only rarely that Froude could spare the time to give public lectures, but when he did speak he always had something illuminating to say. In February 1864, for example, he gave a discourse at the Royal Institution on *The Science of History,* taking the opportunity of expressing doubt about our ability to predict historical events, which was thought to be possible by some of those who regarded history as an exact science. "Gibbon believed", said Froude, "that the era of conquerors was at an end. Had he lived out the full life of man, he would have seen Europe at the feet of Napoleon. But a few years ago we believed the world had grown too civilized for war, and the Crystal Palace in Hyde Park was to be the inauguration of a new era. Battles, bloody as Napoleon's, are now the familiar tale of every day; and the arts which have made the greatest progress are the arts of destruction."

In 1869 Froude was elected Lord Rector of the University of St. Andrews. He described this honour as the first public recognition that he had received. In his Rectorial Address he paid a striking tribute to the Scots. He said, "In the first place you are Scots; you come of a fine stock, and much will be expected of you. If we except the Athenians and the Jews, no people so few in number have scored so deep a mark in the world's history as you have done.

"For shrewdness of head, thorough-going completeness, contempt of compromise, and moral backbone, no set of people ever started into life more generously provided. You did not make these things; it takes many generations to breed high qualities either of mind or body; but you have them, and they are a fine capital to commence business with."

Later in his address he gave a sharp criticism of a type of education still far too common. He said that, "To cram a lad's mind with infinite names of things which he never handled, places he never saw or will see, statements of facts which he cannot possibly understand, and must remain merely words to him—this, in my opinion, is like loading his stomach with marbles; for bread giving him a stone. It is wonderful what a quantity of things of this kind a quick boy will commit to memory, how smartly he will answer questions, how he will show off in school inspections, and delight the heart of his master. But what has been gained for the boy himself, let him carry this kind of thing as far as he will, if, when he leaves school, he has to make his own living?"

He continued, "I accept without qualification the first principle of our forefathers, that every boy born into the world should be put in the way of maintaining himself in honest

independence. No education which does not make this its
first aim is worth anything at all. A man must learn to stand
upright upon his own feet, to respect himself, and to be independent of charity or accident. It is only on this basis that any
superstructure of intellectual cultivation worth having can possibly be built."

The English in Ireland appeared in three volumes between
1871 and 1874. Froude had paid a number of lengthy visits to
Ireland, and was well acquainted with the country and its people.
The object of the book was to oppose Gladstone's policy of
conciliation towards Ireland, and to show that only by the strong
hand could she be made a prosperous country and a tolerable
neighbour. In December 1873, he wrote to a friend: "I am
working hard to finish my Irish book, which I have grown to
hate. It will make the poor Paddies hate me too, which I do not
wish, as I cannot return the feeling." In fact he had every good-
will towards the Irish, but offended them by his temperamental
inability to disguise unfavourable features or to corrupt veracity.

Early in 1875 Froude was invited by Lord Carnarvon to visit
South Africa on a confidential mission to ascertain the state of
political feeling there. Other travels followed to Australia and
elsewhere. The first literary outcome of these experiences was his
Oceana, or England and her Colonies, in 1886. The public was
appreciative, and 75,000 copies were sold within twelve months.
In 1888 there followed *The West Indies or the Bow of Ulysses.*

In 1876 Froude and Professor Huxley were made members
of the Scottish Universities Commission, an appointment which
caused them to pay frequent visits to Edinburgh for several
years afterwards. They were both brilliant talkers, and Skelton*
used to arrange little dinner parties for them. As the aim was
to keep these evenings quite informal and between friends, the
injunction was "not to dress", in response to which Huxley
wrote on one occasion proposing to come in a kilt, "to be as little
dressed as possible". While in the Scottish capital Froude often
stayed at Braid Hermitage with Skelton, who speaks with deep
appreciation of his steadfast friendship through the years.

Froude was on friendly terms with the Carlyles, and it has
been suggested, without much foundation, that he was influenced by the elder historian. It is true that, when Froude

*Sir John Skelton, K.C.B., LL.D.

had had some of the earliest chapters of his history set in type, Carlyle was among the friends to whom they were sent for criticism. Destructive criticism was a congenial occupation for Carlyle, especially as he felt sour disapproval for Froude's patriotism. In one passage of the history there is a description of the English volunteers at Calais who "were for years the terror of Normandy", and of Englishmen in general as "the finest people in all Europe", reared on an abundance of "great shins of beef". Sentiments of this kind were too much for Carlyle, who regarded himself as a Scot, although his name suggests that he was a renegade Englishman. "This", he said, "seems to me exaggerated; what we call John-Bullish. The English are not, in fact, stronger, braver, truer, or better than the other Teutonic races: they never fought better than the Dutch, Prussians, Swedes, etc., have done. For the rest modify a little: Frederick the Great was brought up on beer-sops (bread boiled in beer), Robert Burns on oatmeal porridge; and Mohomet and the Caliphs conquered the world [sic] on barley meal." Froude disregarded the criticism, and left the passage unaltered. How his heart would have been stirred if he could have foreseen the almost incredible heroism of our air pilots in the Battle of Britain.

Having been appointed at a later date Carlyle's literary executor, Froude edited his *Reminiscences* in 1881, a three-volume edition of Mrs. Carlyle's *Letters* in 1882, and a four-volume edition of Carlyle's own *Life* between 1882 and 1884. In preparing this extensive material Froude had a difficult choice to make. The Carlyle household had been queer, gloomy, unhappy, loveless and full of harsh antagonisms for many years. Carlyle had placed his most intimate private papers in Froude's hands before his death, and had stressed that he wished them to be used by his biographer without any reservation or suppression. Mrs. Carlyle likewise had full confidence in his judgment. It fitted in well with Froude's own nature to be encouraged in this way to give the full facts. On the other hand the public was then more conventional than it has since become, and in particular liked its famous men to be wrapped in a sentimental aura of respectability, whatever their private life might really be.

Froude chose the less popular course, and, at the risk of offending admirers of Carlyle, set down the truth bluntly. The

K

resulting biography is one of the world's greatest. Unfortunately relatives of Carlyle, finding many of the revelations
unpalatable, sought vainly to show that the biographer was on
the one hand inaccurate, and on the other that he was publishing
without permission. Froude, who had acted from the highest
motives, was much hurt by these attacks.

In 1892 Froude received an invitation from the Prime
Minister, Lord Salisbury, to become Regius Professor of Modern
History at Oxford, in succession to Freeman. He accepted, in
spite of his advanced years, and took a house at Cherwell Edge,
near the well-known bathing-place called Parson's Pleasure.

The lectures Froude gave at Oxford were attended by crowds
of undergraduates, while those of another historian, Stubbs,
then Bishop of Oxford, a prelate with learning but without
humour, were deserted. The Froude lectures were full of life
and fire. It was said he made more impression on the students
in a few months than Stubbs had done in as many years. His
discourses were felt to be landmarks in the intellectual life of
the university, and the young men who came to hear him
brought away not merely dry facts but fructifying ideas that
inspired a love of learning. But the historian worked so hard
to give his best that he shortened his life.

The Oxford lectures were published in three volumes, and
we are therefore able to see how attractive and interesting they
were. These books were *The Life and Letters of Erasmus*
which appeared in 1894, the *Elizabethan Seamen of the Sixteenth Century*, published in 1895, and the *Lectures on the
Council of Trent*, which came out in 1896. The great amount of
highly concentrated material in these works, and the acute
thought displayed, make them a remarkable final achievement
for a man who had already had such a long and industrious
life. It has been said with justice that if he had been appointed
to his chair twenty years earlier he would have made Oxford
the most famous history school in Europe.

The charm of Froude's company was always irresistible, and
he was very popular both with the university authorities and
with the undergraduates. "Some of the old Dons", he wrote,
"have been rather touchingly kind." He thoroughly understood
the students and enjoyed entertaining them. Although still
young in spirit, however, the strain of such an active life was

serious for a man who had reached the age of seventy-four at the time of his appointment.

At the end of the academic year in 1894 Froude was exhausted and ill. He went to Devon hoping that the sea and the open air would restore him, but the weather proved exceptionally cold and wet, so that he was kept crouching over a fire as storms raged outside and the days of the summer vacation slipped away. His health grew worse under these conditions, and he died at Salcombe in October 1894. He was buried close to the sea he loved.

Skelton, as one of the historian's closest friends, says of him that he was sometimes described as taciturn and saturnine, but that no two words could be less descriptive. He was a singularly vivacious companion, and when he unbent in congenial society would talk vividly on a wide variety of topics. Sometimes, however, he would be severe, for he had a very high standard of right and wrong. He hated all shams, religious, literary and political. The casuistry of the rhetorician, the sophistical make-believe of the worldly ecclesiastic, he could not abide: in public as in private they were abhorrent to him. But while he had a passionate scorn of meanness and truckling, he had an equally passionate reverence for truth, whatever guise it assumed. Although strangers were apt to regard him as reserved and cynical, there was behind the mask an almost tremulous sensitiveness, and a tenderness easily wounded.

In appearance he was striking and impressive. His massive features were strongly lined, yet capable of the subtlest play of expression. His eyes were coal-black and full of lustre: Dr. John Brown, after Froude had given his Rectorial Address at St. Andrews, said: "What a noble utterance that was and is— as full of genius as are his eyes—the glow from within." His black hair was only streaked with grey in his last years. Fortunately admirable likenesses of him have been preserved, as in the portrait by Sir George Reid.

THE HISTORICAL WORKS OF FROUDE
WITH DATES OF PUBLICATION

1852   *England's Forgotten Worthies.*

1856-69 *The History of England from the Fall of Cardinal Wolsey to the Spanish Armada.*

1864   *The Science of History.*

1872-74 *The English in Ireland in the Eighteenth Century.*

1879   *Caesar.*
1886   *Oceana, or England and her Colonies.*
1888   *The English in the West Indies.*
1891   *The Divorce of Catherine of Aragon.*
1891   *Beaconsfield.*
1892   *The Spanish Story of the Armada.*
1894   *The Life and Letters of Erasmus.*
1895   *Elizabethan Seamen of the 16th Century.*
1896   *Lectures on the Council of Trent.*

JOHN RICHARD GREEN
from the engraving by G. J. Stodart

CHAPTER X

John Richard Green
(1837-1883)

"A gradual entering into the spirit of the highest thought the world has ever produced enables us rightly to know what the value of all work, and our work among it, really is."

The earlier essay on W. H. Prescott was written partly as an expression of admiration for great historical work produced under the affliction of partial blindness. There is a close parallel in the life of John Richard Green, whose study of history was undertaken in spite of the suffering inseparable from a disease which in middle-life proved fatal. Few men have equalled the quiet courage of the spirit that Green displayed.

Green was born in Oxford on 12 December 1837. The maiden name of his mother was Hurdis, and it is believed that she was related to the Hurdis who was professor of poetry at Oxford in the eighteenth century, and who wrote in the style of Cowper. He had an uncle, John Green, living in the town, who had literary tastes and lent him books during his boyhood. He very early had a passion for books, and in later years recalls this as characteristic of his childhood, equally with a morbid shyness and a sense of being weaker and smaller than other boys. But W. G. Addison remarks that although Green was weak in physique, he was morally tough. "If I fail," the historian once said, "I have at any rate fought", and this was his attitude from the beginning.

His father was a man of fine character, who was determined to obtain the best education possible for his children, in spite of lack of means. Green says of him: "We were poor, but he was resolved that I should have a good education; and if I have done anything in the world since, it is to that resolve of his that I owe it. I can never honour him too much, for his whole thought was of his children."

The boy was entered at Magdalen College School at the age of eight. The school had the advantage at that time of being within the College precincts, and was like a new world to Green. The College seemed a poem in itself, with its dim cloisters, its noble chapel, its smooth lawns, and its park with the deer browsing beneath venerable elms. He says that of all the Oxford colleges it is the stateliest and the most secluded from the outer world.

Green took great delight in the May morning celebrations at Magdalen. Since the time of Elizabeth a hymn to the Trinity had been sung at dawn on that day from the College tower, while far below the choristers and singing men lay the city enveloped in mist. Green tells of the long hush of waiting just before five and says that, as the first point of sunlight gleamed out over the horizon, there rose in the stillness the soft pathetic air of the hymn. As it closed the sun was fully up, surplices were thrown off, and with a burst of gay laughter the choristers rushed down the little tower-stair, and flung themselves on the bell-ropes, jangling the bells in rough medieval fashion till the tower shook from side to side. And then, as they were tired, came the ringers; and the jangle died into one of those peals, change after change, which used to cast such a spell over Green's boyhood.

His father died of consumption when Green was fourteen, and in the same year he was removed from Magdalen School, of which he had become the head boy, and placed under a private tutor. In 1854, when he was seventeen, his tutor thought it desirable to give him some practice in examination work. He was sent up to compete for an open scholarship at Jesus College, Oxford, which he unexpectedly won. He was obliged to wait a year before he was old enough to go into residence.

In college Green was neither popular nor happy. Possibly, being sensitive and poor, he found himself having little in common with the other students and accordingly out of sympapthy with them. But there were other reasons: Professor Sir Richard Lodge says: "The choice of a college was probably unfortunate; the members of Jesus College were mostly Welshmen, and they were rather isolated from the rest of the university." Green regarded himself as being among foreigners, which was an accurate interpretation of the position, and this was one of the things that led him to withdraw too much into himself. Although of a very kindly nature he quickly acquired a strong

antipathy to Welshmen, and except for his friend "Dax", afterwards Sir William Boyd Dawkins, seems to have had no intimates among his contemporaries. What was more serious,
however, was that he also became hostile to the authorities of
his college.

Green was a man of marked individuality of temperament,
and did not willingly accept conventional restrictions of any
kind, even when to do so would have been helpful to him in
his career. Before going into residence at Jesus College he had
already become keenly interested in history, and had read the
Decline and Fall of the Roman Empire with enthusiasm. It
would have been natural, therefore, for him to have read
History, but he would not do so because at that time the subject
was a conjoint study with Law, for which he had a very under-
standable dislike. In addition, having exceptional maturity of
mind, he could not accept the system then ruling in the History
school, under which the undergraduates worked up selected
passages, and seldom read any books that were not put into their
hands by their tutors. Such methods were perhaps helpful to
less advanced students, but Green felt that in his case the
restrictions would be intolerable. But the price he had to pay
for his independence was a high one for, as Sir John Marriott has
remarked: "Oxford does not lightly forgive the sons who, like
Gibbon and Green, condemn her methods."

Largely from his own choice Green was temperamentally
adrift for his first two years at the university. "I came up to
Oxford," he says, "a hard reader and a passionate High Church-
man; two years of residence left me idle and irreligious. I
rebelled doggedly against the systems around me: I tore myself
from the history which I loved, and plunged into the trifles of
archaeology, because they had no place in the university course."
Then, by good fortune, he heard the famous Dean Stanley say
that: "If you cannot, or will not, work at the work which Oxford
gives you, at any rate work at something." This great principle
came as a revelation to Green, who wrote afterwards: "I took up
my old boy-dream, history, again. I think I have been a steady
worker ever since." In his third year, therefore, we find him
ardently pursuing historical studies, and publishing the first
fruits of them in the Oxford Chronicle. Even as a youth he
had eagerly absorbed the traditions of Oxford, and especially of

Magdalen College, besides being emotionally alive to the atmosphere of the place.   The brilliant essays written in his last year of residence show clearly that his early reading led him in the direction of his later work.   Even at this stage we can trace the methods which he used so successfully as a historian.   He already shows how geographical aspects affect local history, and how local phenomena explain historical events.   He paints lively pictures of eighteenth-century Oxford, and in the modern spirit places emphasis on the social life and everyday things of the past.

Throughout his life Green had the keenest possible interest in the history of Oxford, which arose partly through his affection for it as his birthplace.   The Oxford Historical Society has always recognized that the idea of its formation was due to him. It seemed to him that the past lived here, and that in Oxford it was not possible to maintain the conventional distinction between ancient and modern history.   He wrote in this connection that : "Oxford seems to me the one place where this distinction vanishes.   There in its very system of training the old and the new worlds are brought together as they are brought nowhere else."

It became a major undertaking on Green's part to collect materials for a history of Oxford, and he filled many notebooks with details brought together from a wide range of sources.   He published many essays on this favourite subject in the *Oxford Chronicle,* the *Saturday Review,* and *Macmillan's Magazine.* In the last mentioned journal appeared his account of *Oxford and its Early History,* of which, he says, "the thesis is two-fold : (1) That the University killed the City; and (2) that the Church pretty well killed the University."

In the course of a letter from Italy to one of his friends Green shows how occupied his mind was with this subject of local history.   He writes: "Roaming through these little Ligurian towns makes me utter just the old groans you used to join in when we roamed about France—groans, I mean, over the state of our local histories in England.   There isn't one of these wee places, that glimmer in the night like fireflies in the depth of their bays, that hasn't a full and generally admirable account of itself and its doings.   They are sometimes wooden enough in point of style and the like, but they use their archives, and don't omit, as all our local historians seem to make a point of doing, the history of the town itself.   I have made a little beginning for that of Oxford in the first paper I sent to George Grove; but clearly the first part of such work, the printing and sifting of materials, falls properly to the local antiquary."

In 1901 the Oxford Historical Society published Green's *Studies in Oxford History* in a handsome volume, and in the same year Macmillan & Co. issued in attractive form a shorter selection of his *Oxford Studies*, edited by his widow and his disciple Miss Kate Norgate. How fortunate Oxford was that such a devoted and brilliant son should do her honour.

Upon leaving the university some difficulty was experienced by Green in choosing a profession. His final decision was to take orders. He was ordained in 1860, and at his own wish became a curate in the East End of London. Inherited consumption became evident but he refused to spare himself in the slightest degree, and for eight years laboured for the good of humanity in his chosen sphere. At the end of that time his health was completely ruined and his doctors gave him only six months to live.

As a minister Green was extremely successful. His personal influence with the poor was remarkable, and his sympathy for them unbounded. For years he spent more than his total income from the Church in charity, supporting himself by writing at night, for he had no private means. Through Professor A. E. Freeman he was introduced to the editor of the *Saturday Review*, and contributed articles and reviews to that journal for a period of nearly seven years. His first essay appeared on 2 March 1867, and the last on 10 January 1874. These essays, besides serving the immediate purpose of earning money, paved the way to the full scale writing of history. He became an excellent essayist, and the literary discipline which he imposed upon himself was valuable experience. Most of the work was later reprinted in book form, especially in the *Stray Studies* of 1876, edited by Green himself, and in the volume of *Historical Studies* published in 1903, after his death, and edited by Mrs. Green.

The heavy demands of a poor and hungry parish left Green with little time to himself, but he used the opportunity of being in London to undertake research into early English history at the British Museum. At this time his favourite scheme was for a history of England under Angevin kings, an undertaking only abandoned when his health broke down.

While in charge of the parish of St. Philip's, Stepney, he fought with characteristic energy a terrible outbreak of cholera. He worked day and night in the hospitals and among the panic-stricken poor. An important result of Green's labours in the East End was the influence they exerted on his literary work. He was given a first-hand insight into the lives of the people which was of inestimable value to him. Knowing their life intimately he was enabled to become their spokesman.

Shortly after his thirty-second birthday Green was examined by Dr. Andrew Clark, who found that serious harm had been done to his right lung, damage which would require the greatest care to overcome, if indeed that were still possible. It was necessary to reconcile himself to the life of an invalid and to resign his living. He observed, "I daresay that with patience and care I shall be patched up; but 'patience and care'! Life has never been very amusing, and now it will be greyer and duller than ever." He added that his only regret was that he had not done more in his life, if it was to be a short one.

The resignation of his living was a step that had been in Green's mind quite apart from the breakdown of his health, and it is clear that he would not in any case have remained in the clerical profession. His views had from the first been very broad, and he was constitutionally incapable of insincerity. He became more and more aware, therefore, of his lack of sympathy with obsolete dogmas and the general policy of the Church.

One criticism he made a year or two before this was upon the Church's attitude towards education. He believed that reform in England and in English politics was in many instances impossible because of the want of education among the people. The Church was at that time very much opposed to any national system of education. Green remarked: "The clergy know that a thoroughly educated people, and that people without any uneducated class, would be the ruin of their establishment. And so they fight every point. They won't win in the long run,—but I am sick of looking forward to a free England which will appear about a century and a half after I am dead." He continued with a curiously modern opinion of America, "And so more and more I can't help looking to the West. There is the world as the world will be."

In a letter to a friend in which he expresses resignation to his new lot there is this charming passage: "What seems to grow fairer to me as life goes by is the love and peace and tenderness of it; not its wit and cleverness and grandeur of knowledge, grand as knowledge is, but just the laughter of little children and the friendship of friends, and the cosy talk by the fireside, and the sight of flowers and the sound of music."

Before Green discovered how ill he was, he had intended after leaving the Church to earn a living by writing for the *Saturday*, but to devote most of his time and energy to his study of the Angevin period. The medical verdict he had received made it necessary for him to change this plan. The state of his lungs forced him to curtail his work, and to abandon the project of writing at length on a special period. Instead he decided to give most of the limited hours allowed him by medical advice to preparing the history of the English people, for which his experience and long researches had been such an excellent preparation. He made the following record: "So to live, and also partly that I may set down a few notions which I have conceived concerning history, I have offered Macmillan to write a *Short History of the English People*, 600 pages octavo, which might serve as an introduction to better things if I lived, and might stand for some work done if I didn't. He has taken it, giving me £350 down and £100 if 2,000 copies sell in six months after publication." As regards this agreement it is worthy of note that when the book proved a success, Alexander Macmillan gave Green very generous new terms.

Just as Green found one good Scottish friend in his publisher, so he found another in his Archbishop. Early in 1869 he was appointed to the Lambeth Librarianship by Dr. Archibald Campbell Tait. There was no salary, but rich opportunities for the scholar to conduct research among the great treasures preserved in that famous Library. Green remained Librarian until May 1877. The choice seems to have been a singularly happy one in every way, for the historian brought to his duties much social charm.

When the historian visited some of the ancient towns of the Continent his mind was deeply stimulated. Lord Bryce gives this recollection of a visit to Troyes: *

* *Studies in Biography*, p. 153.

Green had reached the town of Troyes early one morning with two companions, and immediately started off to explore it, darting hither and thither through the streets like a dog trying to find a scent. In two or three hours the examination was complete. The friends lunched together, took the train on to Basel, got there late, and went off to bed. Green, however, wrote before he slept, and laid on the breakfast table next morning an article on Troyes in which its characteristic features were brought out and connected with its fortune and those of the Counts of Champagne during some centuries, an article which was really a history in miniature.

In such cases there was a vigorous interaction between the author and the environment in which he found himself. His previous knowledge of history illuminated vividly the scenes he visited, while at the same time his surroundings threw new light on historical problems. In the *Short History*, and indeed in all his work, Green made admirable use of geographical and archaeological data. He saw clearly the immense effect that these features have had on the history of countries and even villages. His letters contain frequent references to visits made with the object of studying historic remains and of examining the geographical characteristics of the country on the spot. And he was not concerned solely with matters relating to his great undertaking. He had wide interests, and R. Woodman Wadsworth remarks how keenly sensitive he was to beauty and to the more human aspects of nature.

The writing of the *Short History* occupied five years. The record of these years shows a constant and noble struggle against increasing physical disability. Sir William Boyd Dawkins expressed the view that it was undoubtedly interest in his work that kept Green alive, and that but for his history he would have died ten years before he did. He was unable to face English winters, and while abroad was cut off from the most useful sources of reference. He spent three winters in Italy, to which country he became greatly attached.

In visiting Italian cities Green experienced the same delight that so many of his countrymen have felt in the study of these treasuries of the past. On his first visit he saw Ravenna, and left a description of the town which is strangely reminiscent of Ely. He speaks of the great churches standing forgotten in the grey marshes only bounded by the pine-forest and the sea, and of every monument there being literally as old as Hengist.

During the months of each year that Green spent in Italy he wrote many delightful letters to his friends at home. The literary value of his letters is very high, and he had unusual powers of giving vivid little descriptions of out-of-the-way events. Thus, as the following example shows, he could tell a complete story of Italian life for the benefit of a correspondent in just a few lines.

Love and the Madonna—those are the two spiritual sides of the life of a Caprese. I have just been shaking hands through the grating of the Town-prison on the Piazza with a young sailor, who came back to find his loved one coming out of Church from her betrothal with a wealthy old contadino. He stabbed them both; but both are about again—only the contadino thinks better of his intention, and the *inamorata* comes penitently to the prison gate to weep out her repentance, and pour kisses on Giovanni's hand,—the hand that stabbed her. He is a quiet, nice, respectable young fellow, and will soon be out again and marry Carmella, and buy a fishing boat and be a respectable father,—die perhaps a Churchwarden, who knows? At any rate, public opinion goes quite with Giovanni, and I go as I always go—with public opinion.

As the story indicates he was at that time living in Capri, which he thought of making his permanent home. Though sometimes talking of settling in Italy he had a constant wish to be in England. Time and again this longing forms the subject of his letters. Yet Capri had the advantage of being wonderfully cheap. Green found that he could take a comfortable house there, keep two good servants, have a pleasant garden, and spend under £200 a year. At the inn he was charged six francs a day, equivalent to four shillings, for a good room, board and lights. His servant, he found, would count herself rich if he gave her board and ten francs a month, or about eight shillings.

Green felt that it was cowardly to think of marrying when he could only live in sunshine. Writing to an intimate friend who is about to marry he says: "Isn't it very odd to conceive of life without the hope of wife or child, or the stress of public effort or ambition, or any real faith in a hereafter? That is my life." On another occasion he remarks humorously: "The artists here have a way of marrying Caprese donkey-girls and the like, and perhaps I might aspire to a donkey-girl. As to beauty she would be perfect. I know half a dozen donkey-girls who are more beautiful than any English-woman I ever saw."

Green's sense of humour was delicious. Once at San Remo he announced that the following day he was going to High Mass, inasmuch as Catholicism had an organ and Protestantism only a harmonium, and the difference of truth between them didn't seem to him to make up for the difference of instruments. Levity of this kind was not uncommon with him. He was told that in America a popular preacher got £1,500 a year clear, with all paid. "But," said his informant, "you would have to swallow our canons, you know!" Green was understood to say that for £1,500 a year he would swallow all the artillery in America!

Green paid a visit to Garibaldi and describes his memory of the bare, bricked-floored room, the camp bed, the worn homely face, so grand in its utter simplicity, the simple chatty address, all softened with the weariness of pain, the quiet kindly look of the small bright eyes into which a light—such a light—stole once as the veteran recalled a kind act of "you English, who have always been so good to me".

From the references made in the *Short History* alone it is abundantly obvious that Green had a singularly complete knowledge of what was best in English literature. He speaks somewhere of re-reading "Paradise Lost", and being struck with the great inequality of the poem. He goes on: "But I felt more and more the vast force which sweeps together into one great stream all the raised current of Milton's mind, his youthful memories of the romances of chivalry, the recollections of his Italian journeys, his general and rather odd reading, and all that legendry and Talmudic lore which has become so familiar to us that, as in his whole story of the Battle of the Fallen Angels with God, half England believes it to be somewhere in the Bible."

Green was not without that realization of his own powers which most great writers appear to have possessed. He said once that he would never be content till he had superseded Hume, and that he believed he would supersede him, not because he was so good a writer, but because, being an adequate writer, he had a larger and grander conception than Hume of the organic life of a nation as a whole. He said that everything he had written in reviews and essays went to the same point, to a protest, that is, against the tendency to a merely external political view of human affairs, and to a belief that political history to be intelligible and just must be based on social history in its largest sense. Looking through early notes he says he finds the same conviction that one must study men's lives and thoughts and feelings as a necessary condition of judging their political acts. He hoped that his first works would show this, and that if he lived he would be able to make them better and better; if he did not, he would have had his say, even if with "stammering lips".

The number of essays he had written before seeking to work on the *Short History* was very great. He observes that all through the earlier part of that work he saw the mark of the essayist, the tendency to "little vignettes", the jerkiness, and a want of grasp of the subject as a whole. He says, I learnt my trade as I wrote on; a different sort of work begins with Edward I: but it is not till I reach the new learning that I feel a freedom from that fatal essayism."

The first part of the *Short History* was written at Minster in the Isle of Thanet. Green complains in February 1870, he was then thirty-two, of finding it horrible work to condense the English Conquest into five pages and the Conversion into six and yet be interesting, but he thinks that he had managed pretty well. The following month his small reserve of strength was exhausted and he speaks of spitting blood and being depressed and weary. He records that he was doing some work every day, but that it was very hard when one was weak and disheartened. More than once he speaks of the great deal of work he had put into what he had done, and of having re-written passages again and again to get them to his liking. On another occasion he remarked: "Remember my theory of life is no mere indolence theory. I have worked hard and mean to work hard on things which have a worthy end and use."

When he had only about a chapter and a half to do, so far as writing went, Green turned his attention for a short time to chronological tables and maps, both of which he declared he disliked intensely. He suggested amusingly that he had thoughts of putting in anything—say the map of Abyssinia, lettering it beneath, "Very Early England indeed", and so on.

The purpose that Green had in mind in writing his history is well expressed in the preface. In it he says: "The aim of the following work is defined by its title; it is a history, not of English Kings or English Conquests, but of the English People. At the risk of sacrificing much that was interesting and attractive in itself, and which the constant usage of our historians has made familiar to English readers, I have preferred to pass lightly and briefly over the details of foreign wars and diplomacies, the personal adventures of kings and nobles, the pomp of courts, or the intrigues of favourites, and to dwell at length on the incidents of that constitutional, intellectual and social advance in which we read the history of the nation itself. It was with this purpose that I have devoted more space to Chaucer than to Cressy, to Caxton than the petty strife of Yorkist and Lancastrian, to the Poor Law of Elizabeth than to her victory at Cadiz, to the Methodist revival than to the escape of the young Pretender. Whatever the worth of the present work may be, I have striven throughout that it should never sink into a 'drum and trumpet' history."

The freshness of Green's point of view made his history specially valuable. It had become the conventional habit to regard certain types of event as worthy of inclusion in historical works, but to exclude others that in truth were of equal importance. It may now seem that Green went from one extreme to another and that the *Short History* was no better proportioned than the works of the earlier historians, but he achieved much in keeping an open mind and in breaking the fetters of convention with which a great deal of historical literature had become bound. One of those who has followed to some extent in the tradition established by Green is G. M. Trevelyan. The novelty of Green's approach was noticeable even in such details as the discarding of the division of the history into reigns, which until his day had been practically the universal custom.

The *Short History* revealed for the first time the full significance of the great social movements in our history. As a whole it is remarkable for the dramatic force of the narrative, in spite of great conciseness in expression on account of its short length. Perhaps full justice is not done in it to the Tudor Kings, particularly Henry VIII, who by diverting a handsome part of the revenues of the monasteries to the universities did more for the

cause of education in this country than any other single individual, and who by his encouragement and protection of trade
advanced our commercial greatness.   But in some ways his
narrative gained in strength from the very fact that he pursued his course with a certain relentless purpose that caused
him to disregard anything that did not fit in with his general
scheme.

The *Short History of the English People* appeared towards
the end of 1874, and met with a very cordial reception.   Bryce
said the book was "philosophical enough for scholars, and
popular enough for schoolboys".   The work was an unparalleled
success, for 150,000 copies were sold within fifteen years of
publication.   The book was quickly reprinted in America, but
as copyright at that time was almost non-existent in the States,
Green received no benefit from the large sales there.   One day
about this time he writes: "I am musing gloomily on the Pirate
Copy which has arrived from New York, gorgeous in form, and
margin, and type, a fine book, but a Felon!   As I look on it
my dream of a brougham fades away and I fall back on the
chance of a market-cart to jog through life with."

After the publication of his history Green was in somewhat
easier circumstances and was able to see more of his friends.
Sometimes, for example, he visited his fellow-historian Freeman
at Somerleaze, the latter's estate in Somerset.   Wells and
Glastonbury were close at hand and on one occasion Green
writes: "I earwigged the organist at the Cathedral and got him
to play me a lot of Mendelssohn's organ music after everybody
was gone, the great Cathedral seemed so grand when one was all
alone there with the music rolling away down the nave."

In January 1877 Green became engaged to Alice, daughter
of the Venerable E. A. Stopford, Archdeacon of Meath.   In
one of his letters to her he refers to the *Short History* in the
following terms: "I shall do far better work before I die; but
there is a fire, an enthusiasm in one's first book that never comes
again."

The revision and expansion of the *Short History,* to form the
basis of the much larger *History of the English People,* was
made exceedingly difficult by the necessity which Green faced of
wintering abroad.   He did in fact cause large cases of books to
be transported for him to southern Italy, but the volumes made

L

available to him in this way were only a small fraction of those he needed. Nothing could compensate for being cut off from the charters, calendars and other historical documents preserved in the Record Office, the British Museum and the other great London Libraries. During the last summers he was able to spend in London he had to work not only against ill-health, but also against time. The strain, therefore, was extremely heavy, and would have broken a man whose spirit was less gallant. After his betrothal to Miss Stopford he mentions this feature of his work to her in a letter of which the following is an extract: "I *must* get the work I am doing finished up to Elizabeth's day in the next fortnight, because I can't take abroad the huge calendars I need for that period. . . . I am very tired and weary too, and my work presses on me as it has seldom done, but I go doggedly on." It is evident all the time how he was sustained by his passion for historical investigation.

Five months after his engagement Green married, believing himself to be in better health. A few weeks later he had an attack of haemorrhage, and remarks: "It is strange how in a single night all strength seems to ebb out of me and to leave me next morning helpless and feverish on a sofa." He had to fight at these times against mental depression, and says: "I felt the old feeling of disappointment of life waking up again, and carrying me back into the old grey dead hopelessness." To others, however, nothing of this weariness was evident. When he and his wife visited Tennyson, the poet said to him: "You're a jolly, vivid man, and I'm glad to have known you; you're as vivid as lightning." Green's marriage was entirely happy, and he was greatly helped by his wife's understanding and sympathy in the short time he had yet to live. Mrs. Green was many years his junior, and a woman of great beauty.

The *History of the English People* was published in four volumes in 1878-80, but in spite of careful revision of earlier matter it is not nearly so well known as the shorter work. Even then Green's labours were not at an end. He began to write a history on the largest scale from an existing fragment of which it is possible at least to estimate the extraordinary amount of research that had been undertaken to produce the *Short History*. Of this major project he completed the first volume, on *The Making of England*, in time for publication in January 1882.

The second volume, on *The Conquest of England* was published posthumously, after having been completed by Mrs. Green. It is a tragedy that the premature death of the historian, which nowadays could probably have been avoided by the greater scope of medical science, robbed the world of the realization of Green's grand conception of our history.

Before the end Green enjoyed some recognition of his work. Thus in 1879 the University of Edinburgh conferred the degree of LL.D. upon him, Scotland being, as ever, appreciative of learning. Bishop Stubbs says: "Green possessed in no scanty measure all the gifts that contribute to the making of a great historian. He combined, so far as the history of England is concerned, a complete and firm grasp of the subject in its unity and integrity, with a wonderful command of detail and a thorough sense of perspective and proportion. All his work was real and original work; few people besides those who knew him well would see, under the charming ease and vivacity of his style, the deep research and sustained industry of the laborious student. But is was so; there was no department of our national records that he had not studied, and I think I may say mastered. And then, to add still more to the debt we owe him, there is the wonderful simplicity and beauty of the way he tells his tale."

Green's health grew worse. For a while he was still able to see his friends and talk with them. Mrs. Humphrey Ward says: "There in the corner of the sofa sat the thin wasted form, life flashing from the eyes, breathing from the merry or eloquent lips, beneath the very shadow and seal of death—the eternal protesting life of the intelligence. Mr. Green's was talk of the best kind; his poet's instinct for the lives and thoughts of others, his quick imagination, his humorous and human curiosity about all sorts and sides of things, made pose and pedantry impossible to him."

Green continued his work gallantly until the end. A few months before his death he wrote while suffering deeply: "There is nothing for it but patience and good humour; but it is sometimes hard to feel one's brain as active as ever and yet doomed to inaction from being chained to this 'body of death', as Paul called it long ago." He died in Mentone on 7 March 1883, at the early age of forty-five.

THE HISTORICAL WORKS OF GREEN
WITH DATES OF PUBLICATION

1874   *A Short History of the English People.*

1876   *Stray Studies.*

1878-80   *The History of the English People* (4 Vols.)

1882   *The Making of England.*

1883   *The Conquest of England (posthumous publication).*

1901   *Studies in Oxford History (posthumous publication).*

1903   *Historical Studies (posthumous publication).*

SIR WINSTON CHURCHILL
from the portrait by Professor Arthur Pan

CHAPTER XI

Sir Winston Churchill, K.G.

(Born 1874)

In considering Churchill here we are directly concerned only with his record as a historian. Like Clarendon, however, who although famous as a historian, was described by Southey as also "the wisest, most upright of statesmen", the historical writings of Churchill are based on his own long career in the service of the state. In particular, as the greatest war leader his country has ever had, we can with advantage examine his own army career, from subaltern to commanding officer, and observe how he recorded the details of each campaign in which he fought. His histories, always brilliantly written, have gained steadily in authority and nobility of conception, from his account of *The Malakand Field Force,* which appeared in 1898, to his great *History of the English-Speaking Peoples,* publication which was completed in 1958, just sixty years later.

Few men have juster cause to feel pride in their ancestry, and a parallel to Churchill's own distinction can often be found in the achievements of his forebears. There is, for example, a literary tradition in the family which dates back at least to the time of the Sir Winston Churchill whose work entitled, *Divi Britannici: being a Remark on all the Kings of this Isle,* was printed by Thomas Roycroft in 1675.

Quite frequently Churchill indulges in a characteristic kind of quip in which a mild and apparently harmless opening is followed by something so shattering that one can only gasp. Once in the Commons, for example, he remarked casually that, "It will be found much better by all parties to leave the past to history", then came the flash of lambent humour as he added, "especially as I propose to write that history myself".

In point of fact there grew in him early a sense of history which played its part in giving his writings and utterances that quality of elevated thought which made them so worthy of great themes and occasions. This faculty became highly developed as through the years he helped to make history. "I do not speak of these matters on the spur of the moment," he reminded Parliament, "but from a steady stream of thought which I have followed and pursued with a study and experience of these matters over many years."

There were clear indications of his special tastes and abilities from an early age. At Harrow, which he entered at the age of thirteen, he disliked Latin and mathematics, in both of which he was backward, but showed himself very advanced in English composition. He did not distinguish himself at the school until as a senior he entered the Army Class, when he developed an enthusiasm for military science which he had never had for Latin declensions: as he himself put it, he "could learn quickly enough the things that mattered".

His father intended that Winston should make the army his career, and from Sandhurst, where he had an outstanding record, he was duly commissioned as a "regular". He was extraordinarily keen, and in 1896 obtained a transfer to the Indian Army as the best way of seeing some actual fighting. It proved impossible to keep him away from any action that was taking place. In the next four years he fought in four wars, in Asia, Africa and South America, collecting "a phenomenal number of medals for daring in action". In his book *My Early Life* he describes with gusto some of his adventures and hairbreadth escapes.

While Churchill was at Poona, very soon after landing in India, he was invited by the Governor, Lord Sandhurst, to a banquet at Government House. The young cavalry subaltern, never lacking in self-possession, enjoyed himself vastly. He says of the occasion: "His Excellency, after the health of the Queen-Empress had been drunk and dinner was over, was good enough to ask my opinion upon several matters, and considering the magnificent character of his hospitality, I thought it would be unbecoming in me not to reply fully. I have forgotten the particular points of British and Indian affairs upon which he sought my counsel; all I can remember is that I responded generously. There were indeed moments when he seemed willing to impart his own views; but I thought it would be ungracious to put him to so much trouble; and he very readily subsided." Eventually an aide-de-camp was sent with the young guest to make sure that he found his way back to camp safely.

But festive occasions were rare, and Winston found many ways of keeping himself constantly occupied. He organized a scratch polo team to such a pitch of efficiency that it defeated all the crack teams and won the All-India Cup. He studied hard also, reading history, philosophy and economics. History was a subject that had a natural appeal for him. He says: "I had always liked history at school. But there we were given only the dullest, driest pemmicanised forms like *The Student's Hume*." He read Macaulay, borrowing a copy of the latter's History from the brother-in-law of his childhood's nurse, an old prison warder who used to speak of it with reverence. Churchill says: "I accepted all Macaulay wrote as gospel, and I was grieved to read his harsh judgments upon the Great Duke of Marlborough." He was only twenty-one at this time, and continues: "There was no one at hand to tell me that this historian, with his captivating style and devastating self-confidence, was the prince of literary rogues, who always preferred the tale to the truth, and smirched or glorified great men, and garbled documents, according as they affected his drama. I cannot forgive him for imposing on my confidence and on the simple faith of my old friend the warder." He continued with historical studies of this kind, reading right through the long glistening middle hours of the Indian day, when he was off duty.

In the course of the studies which Churchill undertook while in India he came to consider religion. He expresses some frank and amusing views. He held that as at Harrow there had been three services every Sunday he had accumulated in his years there so fine a surplus in the Bank of Observance that he had been drawing confidently upon it ever since. In the army too there were regular church parades, and sometimes he marched the Roman Catholics to church, and sometimes the Protestants. He remarks that religious tolerance in the British Army had spread till it overlapped the regions of indifference.

In his regiment some of the senior officers dwelt upon the value of the Christian religion to women—"It helps to keep them straight", and to the lower orders—"Nothing can give them a good time here, but it makes them more contented to think they will get one hereafter." Churchill adds the comment that Christianity, it appeared, had also a disciplinary value, especially when presented through the Church of England. On the other hand too much religion of any kind was a bad thing. Among natives especially, fanaticism was highly dangerous and roused them to murder, mutiny or rebellion.

At Bangalore he read works which challenged the religious education he had received at Harrow. Among these was *The Martyrdom of Man* by Winwood Reade, which he describes as a concise and well-written universal history of mankind, dealing in harsh terms with the mysteries of all religions and leading to the depressing conclusion that we simply go out like candles. To begin with Churchill was much startled and indeed offended by what he read, but then found that Gibbon evidently held the same view. Finally a predominantly secular view was established in his mind by reading Lecky's *Rise and Influence of Rationalism*, and his *History of European Morals*.

At this time, records Winston, "I passed through a violent and aggressive anti-religious phase which, had it lasted, might easily have made me a nuisance". He became tolerant again on the theory that it would be foolish to discard the reasons of the heart for those of the head when he could enjoy them both. It seemed to him to be good to let the mind explore so far as it could the paths of thought and logic, and also good to pray for help and succour, and be thankful when they came. He adds characteristically: "Accordingly I have always been surprised to see some of our Bishops and clergy making such heavy weather about reconciling the Bible story with modern scientific and historical knowledge. Why do they want to reconcile them?"

He remarks that the idea that nothing is true except what we comprehend is silly: "Certainly nothing could be more repulsive both to our minds and feelings than the spectacle of thousands of millions of universes—for that is what they say it comes to now—all knocking about together for ever without any rational or good purpose behind them." So quite early in life he adopted a simple and convenient system of believing whatever he wanted to believe, while leaving reason to pursue its course unfettered.

The first historical work written by Churchill was his *Malakand Field Force*, based upon his experience while on active service in the north-west frontier of India in 1896. In that campaign he was mentioned in despatches by General Sir

Bindon Blood, who praised "the courage and resolution of Lieut. W. L. S. Churchill, 4th Hussars". He took part in a good deal of hand-to-hand fighting with the Pathan tribesmen, in which the British troops suffered considerable losses. His book was written in lively style, and immediately proved a great success, both from a literary and a financial standpoint. The Prince of Wales, afterwards Edward VII, sent him this cordial note of congratulation:

Marlborough House,
April 22nd, 1898.

My Dear Winston,

I cannot resist writing a few lines to congratulate you on the success of your book! I have read it with the greatest possible interest and think the descriptions and the language generally excellent. Everybody is reading it, and I only hear it spoken of with praise. Having now seen active service you will wish to see more, and have as great a chance I am sure of winning the V.C. as Fincastle had; and I hope you will not follow the example of the latter, who I regret to say intends leaving the Army in order to go into Parliament.

You have plenty of time before you, and should certainly stick to the Army before adding M.P. to your name.

Hoping you are flourishing,
I am,
Yours very sincerely,
A. E.

Lord Salisbury, the Prime Minister, asked him to call so that he could tell him personally how much he had enjoyed the book. But part of the merit of the work lay in its lively military criticism. Mistakes had been made in the conduct of the campaign, and Winston exposed them with the first-hand knowledge of the man who had been on the spot. A wit said the book should have been called *A Subaltern's Hints to Generals,* and serious offence was given in high military quarters.

Even so early in his career the author displayed his gift of giving in a few words a striking picture of the scene of the campaign, speaking, for example, of terrain "as tangled as the maze at Hampton Court, with mountains instead of hedges". The *Graphic* said: "No more vivid picture of the recent frontier war has yet been afforded than that given by Mr. Winston Churchill in his vigorously written and intensely interesting narrative." Other press comments were equally favourable. "The book is written with all the freshness and lively observation that might be expected from a clever war correspondent," declared the *Morning Post,* "and these qualities are combined with a commendable faculty for making military movements and tactics understood by the civilian."

To avoid loss of time by having the proofs sent out to him in India, he entrusted the correction of them to an uncle who was himself a writer. Winston makes the comment that for some reason his uncle missed many scores of shocking misprints and made no attempt to organize the punctuation. So although in general reviewers were complimentary, and mentioned such features as, "wisdom and comprehension far beyond his years", a discriminating journal like the *Athenaeum* had a sarcastic reference to "Pages of Napier punctuated by a mad printer's reader".

Winston has this note on the liking which the tribesmen of the Indian frontier had for the breech-loading rifle introduced in the nineteenth century: "The convenience of the breech-loading, and still more of the magazine rifle was nowhere more appreciated than in the Indian highlands. A weapon which would kill with accuracy at fifteen hundred yards opened a whole new vista of delights to every family or clan which could acquire it. One could actually remain in one's own house and fire at one's neighbours nearly a mile away. One could lie in wait on some high crag, and at hitherto unheard-of range hit a horseman far below. Even villages could fire at each other without the trouble of going far from home. Fabulous prices were therefore offered for these glorious products of science. Rifle-thieves scoured all India to reinforce the efforts of the honest smuggler. A steady flow of the coveted weapons spread its genial influence throughout the frontier, and the respect which the Pathan tribesmen entertained for Christian civilization was vastly enhanced."

In writing his accounts of the campaigns in which he took part, Churchill was helped by the fact that he had an arrangement by which he acted as a newspaper correspondent. As a direct consequence of his outspoken reports serving officers are no longer allowed to act in this capacity. While with the North-West frontier expedition he was correspondent for the *Daily*

Telegraph and in the Sudan he wrote for the *Morning Post*. The latter paper was also represented by him in the Boer War. Work of this kind not only gave him practice in writing, but caused him to make a systematic record of events at the time they happened, and provided him with raw materials for his books.

The campaign in the Sudan enabled Winston to see more active service, and as usual he managed to be continually in the middle of the heaviest fighting. He rode with the 21st Lancers at the Battle of Omdurman, thus taking part in one of the last great classic cavalry charges of history, the date being September 1898. The fiercely fought operations freed the Sudan from fanatical power, and brought the whole of the Nile Valley under British influence.

The fighting in the Sudan gave Churchill material for his two-volume work on *The River War,* so named after the Nile. This was the second of his histories, and in it he showed himself strongly critical even of Kitchener, the Commander-in-Chief. The young author expressed himself with real insight and ability, as also with devastating accuracy, so that his literary reputation was enhanced. In a perfect world his military standing would also have been raised greatly, but in the event the generals did not relish instruction, however excellent, from a junior officer, and instead of the rapid promotion which he had earned, strong influence was brought to bear to bring his career in the army to a close.

In addition to the experiences described, Churchill ran fearsome risks in the Spanish War in South America and was awarded the Spanish Order of Military Merit (1st class). But his next opportunity of service in the Empire was when the South African War broke out. The military authorities felt no urgent inclination to make use of the services of Winston in the war, although he tried his utmost to be sent out. But he was not to be denied, and arranged to go as a war correspondent, being one of the first to land in South Africa. In November 1899, an armoured train in which he was travelling in Natal was ambushed by the Boers, and after taking a spirited part in the defence he was taken prisoner. As a correspondent he had no right to join in the fighting, but he naturally found the urge irresistible, and did so much to rally the troops on the train that

when he finally fell into the hands of the Boers they were in two
minds about shooting him.

When Winston had been in an improvised Boer concentration camp for a few weeks he managed to break out. He then
became a hunted man. A proclamation was issued offering a
reward of £25 to "anyone who brings in the escaped prisoner
of war, Churchill, dead or alive". The fugitive was described
in these terms:

Englishman, 25 years old, about 5 ft. 8 ins. tall, indifferent build,
walks with a forward stoop, pale appearance, red-brownish hair, small
and hardly noticeable moustache, talks through his nose and cannot
pronounce the letter 's' properly.

The Boers made tremendous efforts to recapture Churchill,
and the British press became keyed to a high pitch of excitement
as the victim of the man-hunt continued to elude his pursuers.
After remarkable adventures, that constantly demanded great
courage and the utmost presence of mind, Churchill escaped
into Portuguese territory. Upon his return to South Africa he
found himself a national hero (this in 1900!), but his sole
preoccupation was to return to the attack, and in the minimum
of time he was back in the fighting with a commission in the
South African Light Horse. Then until the close of hostilities
he was actively engaged wherever the fighting was heaviest.

The first volume of Churchill's record of the South African
war was entitled, *London to Ladysmith via Pretoria*. *The Times*
said it was "An account given with modest and frank simplicity".
The *Scotsman* expressed the view that it was "One of the most
brilliant narratives of the war in Natal". The *Spectator* said,
"we can heartily recommend Mr. Winston Churchill's book as
one from which a great deal may be drawn for the right understanding of the situation. He has not only a good head for
a political problem, but he has also wonderful eyes to observe
and a fluent pen to record."

Ian Hamilton's March, also published in 1900, was a continuation of the *London to Ladysmith* book. It deals with the
march of General Hamilton's column on the flank of Lord
Roberts's main army from Bloemfontein to Pretoria. This force
overcame the main Boer resistance by fighting ten general
actions and many smaller ones. The work is written from the

point of view of one who was present at every action: "Mr. Churchill's book is unique, because his experiences have been unique." It is not without due cause that a Churchill book is described as, "A stirring record of individual prowess and adventure".

At the end of the South African War the young veteran entered Parliament. His father had died some years before, so that he had to make his way in public life without paternal aid or guidance. How quickly he absorbed the atmosphere of the House, and gained an extensive knowledge of our Parliamentary institutions, is shown by the fact that before long, actuated partly by motives of filial piety, he undertook to write the life of his father. Soon after this work was published he married Miss Clementine Hozier, descended on her mother's side from the Earls of Airlie, whose country seat is close to Dundee, in County Angus, a constituency which he represented for several years.

The *Life of Lord Randolph Churchill* appeared in 1906. This biography of his father ranks high as an eloquent tribute to a man of unusual brilliance whose career was tragically brought to a premature close by his death at the early age of forty-six. In addition it is a vivid account of a chapter in English Parliamentary history, especially between the years 1880 and 1890. Lord Randolph was the leader of the most progressive section of the Conservative party, and if he had lived would no doubt have acquired increasing fame. In the short time available to him, however, he sacrificed much through remaining independent and disinterested. At the close of the biography by his son there is this passage: "There is an England which stretches far beyond the well-drilled masses who are assembled by party machinery to salute with appropriate acclamation the utterances of their recognised fuglemen; an England of wise men who gaze without self-deception at the failings and follies of both political parties; of brave and earnest men who find in neither faction fair scope for the effort that is in them; of 'poor men' who increasingly doubt the sincerity of the party philanthropy. It was to that England that Lord Randolph Churchill appealed; it was that England he so nearly won; it is by that England he will be justly judged."

In 1914 Churchill was anxious to have a command in the field, but as a member of the Government had to remain in

London. Friction grew between him and Asquith, for while, as Lord Beaverbrook remarks, Churchill "possessed a mind singularly adapted to deal with a war of new methods and surprises", his chief had no such qualities. A break came in 1915, and Churchill eagerly took the opportunity of going out to France as a Major in the Grenadier Guards. As a politician he had a cold reception from his brother officers, but quickly earned their liking and respect. When the Second-in-Command went on leave, the Colonel asked him to undertake the duties, which Churchill regarded as a great compliment. A little later, as Lewis Broad says: "Winston secured an impressive report from his Colonel testifying that he had gained exceptional knowledge of trench warfare in all its forms and was fully competent for a command." Early in 1916 he was promoted and given command of a battalion of the Royal Scots.

Professor Dewar Gibb, who served as a Captain in Colonel Churchill's battalion, says of him: "I am firmly convinced that no more popular officer ever commanded troops. As a soldier he was hard-working, persevering and thorough. He was out to work hard at tiresome but indispensable detail and to make his unit efficient in the very highest possible degree. And, moreover, he loved soldiering; it lay very near his heart and I think he could have been a very great soldier." He hated inaction, and soon found ways of relieving the tedium of life in the trenches. Thus he engaged in private wars with the Germans opposite, usually at night. He arranged for his men to put up bursts of rifle and machine-gun fire until the enemy thought something was in the wind and retaliated in kind. Then Colonel Churchill would telephone urgently demanding artillery support because he was being attacked, and there would be a general flare-up in the sector. Neighbouring units that preferred a quiet life did not approve, but Churchill himself, once his nocturnal strafe was in full career, would remark in satisfied tones, "This is great, isn't it?"

The capacity of Churchill in military matters was of such a high order that it could not be overlooked, and in due course he was recalled to G.H.Q. and given a brigade in the division of General Bridge. To what heights Brigadier Churchill might have risen in the service must remain unknown, for he was now to be the victim of a great injustice. Sir John French, who was then Commander-in-Chief, made the appointment the very day before he had to pay a visit to London to see the Premier. When Asquith heard of the promotion he appears to have been jealous and vindictive, and to have used his influence to have it cancelled. It was, of course, wrong of the Premier, as Beaverbrook says, "to interfere for political reasons with the decision of the Commander-in-Chief in France, who judged Churchill's merits as a soldier and thought him worthy of a Brigade". But French was already under the cloud that led to him being superseded, and, lacking the courage to assert himself, he held Churchill's new appointment in suspense. Lord Beaverbrook adds: "My own opinion was that Churchill would have guarded his superior against all kinds of errors both military and diplomatic. One Churchill on his staff might have saved French from dismissal."

At this stage many of Churchill's friends and colleagues in the House of Commons redoubled their pressure to persuade him to resume his Parliamentary duties, and he finally agreed to do so because, through the curious circumstances described, he found himself at G.H.Q. without any immediate prospect of employment, through no fault of his own. He returned to England to help in the direction of the war with the immense advantage of having first-hand knowledge through having taken part in the actual fighting.

In the General Election of 1922 Churchill was not returned to Parliament, being left without a seat for the first time since 1900. In the period that followed he turned again to writing. His full-scale history of the first World War was given the title of *The World Crises, 1911-1918, and the Aftermath,* being published by Thornton Butterworth in five volumes between 1923 and 1929. Of this work *The Times* said that it was, "Written with a vigour and grace, and command of literary art, which no historian of this war has yet approached". The *Daily Telegraph* described it as, "A great piece of literature and the greatest of literary searchlights on the dark confusion of the world conflict". In 1931 he published, as a supplement, his book on *The Eastern Front.*

In the period 1933-38 Churchill worked on his monumental biography of the first Duke of Marlborough, published under the title of *Marlborough, his Life and Times.* The fact that he was out of office enabled him to devote a considerable amount of time to examining the great store of previously untapped manuscript treasures at his birthplace, Blenheim Palace. Much of the actual writing of this work was done in Canada, and it is interesting to observe how cosmopolitan he was in this respect, for the *World Crises* volumes were dictated partly on the Riviera, and when he came to write his account of the second World War he worked in North Africa and elsewhere.

Among biographical studies of historical personages this life of Marlborough takes a leading place. Owen Morshead, librarian to George V, records that when it appeared His Majesty remarked, "There's Winston's life of his ancestor—no doubt everything he did was right! A bit too highbrow for me, I expect, but I shall take it down to Sandringham to have a try; I dare say I shan't get far. Beautiful writer he is and a wonderful good fellow, too, into the bargain."

Long before the second World War we find Churchill established as a true statesman in a Parliament where perhaps only he could rightly claim that title. Before Munich he stressed the need for planes, national service and other preparations to preserve national safety. After Munich he said very bluntly in the Commons: "You were given the choice between war and dishonour. You chose dishonour and you will have war." What more natural than that the nation should turn to such a man for leadership when war had come and peril was grave. In a moving passage he says: "Thus then, on the night of the tenth of May (1940), at the outset of this mighty battle (The Battle of Britain), I acquired the chief power in the State, which henceforth I wielded in evergrowing measure for five years and three months of world war, at the end of which time, all our enemies having surrendered unconditionally or being about to do so, I was immediately dismissed by the British electorate from all further conduct of their affairs."

The extraordinary reversal of fortune which Churchill had in 1945, at least had the advantage that he was set free to write another great historical work, surpassing in scale and grandeur anything he had written previously. He had intended to leave to his heirs his diaries and his vast accumulation of other records, but leisure caused him to change his mind, and in May 1947, it was announced that he was engaged upon his Memoirs.

This news caused a sensation in literary circles, and there was keen competition for the rights of publication. His old friend Lord Camrose, owner of the *Daily Telegraph*, obtained the Empire rights, and acted for him in the United States. The negotiations in America lasted six months, and the contract finally made covered eleven pages, with a price not yet disclosed but estimated at upwards of a million dollars.

In the States it was arranged that there was to be a serialization from early in 1948, in the way of daily instalments in the *New York Times*, and weekly ones in *Life*, with publication in book form afterwards by the firm of Houghton. Churchill's mother was American (through her he was directly descended from George Washington), and it is of interest to note that his grandfather was at one time the proprietor of the *New York Times*. Incidentally much in his character seems to belong to a new country, and one may speculate upon the contribution of his American ancestry to his make-up. Lewis Broad says that "This vigour and versatility belong to earlier generations in our history before the accumulating influences of civilization had worn down the zest of man. Winston Churchill has all the appurtenances of the Elizabethans—their richness, their colour, their freshness. He responds to new inventions and new ideas as did the men of the Renaissance. There is the same glamour about his actions."

Churchill's great work on *The Second World War* is a continuation of his account of the first struggle with Germany, and his declared intention is that together they shall serve as the record of another Thirty Years War. He states that throughout he has followed the method of Defoe's *Memoirs of a Cavalier*, in which the author hangs the chronicle and discussion of great military and political events upon the thread of the personal experiences of an individual. In following this course he had unique advantages, as being perhaps the only man to have passed through what he terms "the two supreme cataclysms of recorded history" while holding high office.

In writing this latter history Churchill was able to make admirable use of the Memoranda, Directives, Personal Telegrams and Minutes which he issued as Prime Minister, and which amounted to nearly a million words. These documents were not only a most valuable continuous contemporary record

M

of the conduct of the war, but express the views of the one who carried the main responsibility for policy and who held the chief executive power.

The first volume bears the title of *The Gathering Storm*, and the date March 1948. The theme of the volume is given as, "How the English-speaking Peoples, through their unwisdom, Carelessness and Good Nature allowed the Wicked to rearm". Book I, *From War to War*, is a review of the period 1919 to 1939. Book II, *The Twilight War*, covers the events that took place between 3 September 1939 and 10 May 1940.

In his masterly survey of the pre-war years Churchill gives a succinct history of the whole of Europe during this period. In these opening sections of the work we feel at once the lofty detachment and impartiality of the great historian, and trace the instinct for the right word and phrase that reveal the true artist. And with what penetrating insight he can sum up in a sentence the views of his contemporaries on a particular subject, as when he says of Baldwin, "He knew little of Europe and disliked what he knew", and of Chamberlain, "Unlike Baldwin, he conceived himself able to comprehend the whole field of Europe and, indeed, the world".

The latter part of the first volume forms an interesting contrast to the earlier part. Instead of the broad European scene we are concerned mainly with his own work at the Admiralty when he returned to office—an event celebrated throughout the Royal Navy by the ships flashing round the joyful message: "Winston is back!" We are given a fascinating view of the problems of naval warfare, and of the bold strategic solutions which he worked out. Often at this time he was not allowed to put his plans into operation: the French, for example, would not agree to mines being dropped in the Rhine, on the principle "Don't be unkind to the enemy, you will only make him angry".

The second volume, *Their Finest Hour*, is dated January 1949. The author gives the theme as, "How the British People held the fort alone, till those who hitherto had been half blind were half ready". Book I deals with *The Fall of France*. Book II, *Alone*, is concerned with the time when "We were alone, with victorious Germany and Italy engaged in mortal attack upon us, with Soviet Russia a hostile neutral actively aiding Hitler, and Japan an unknowable menace. However, the British War

Cabinet, conducting His Majesty's affairs with vigilance and fidelity, supported by Parliament and sustained by the Governments and peoples of the British Commonwealth and Empire, enabled all tasks to be accomplished and overcame all our foes."

To this magnificent theme Churchill does full justice. It has been well said that as war leader he "brought back the arrogance and splendour of Elizabethan language", and that "his words embodied the spirit of England fighting alone". The fineness of his own mind is constantly evident in this record of one of the supreme testing times of our national history. And, besides being a proud and imperishable record of great deeds accomplished, his account will undoubtedly give inspiration to future generations, for his words stir the blood like a clarion call: we are living again in the days of the Armada, and of Richard Grenville and the *Revenge*.

The third volume, *The Grand Alliance*, came out in July 1950, and describes the events of the year 1941, its theme being: "How the British fought on with hardship their garment until Soviet Russia and the United States were drawn into the great conflict." This is the period when desert victory was followed by defeats in Greece and Crete, and when there were major happenings like the Japanese attack on Pearl Harbour and the German thrust against Russia. Churchill says: "I cannot recall any period when the stresses and the onset of so many problems all at once or in rapid succession bore more directly on me and my colleagues than the first half of 1941."

A major historical work like *The Second World War* makes searching demands upon the author, who must have rich resources to draw upon. The more carefully we consider Churchill's achievement the more evident his success is. There are certain overriding features, like his highly individualistic style, which gives a flavour to the whole. Thus no history has been written on quite the same lines, although a partial parallel is to be found in the work of Clarendon. Throughout, too, we meet countless examples of his deep humanity, his dignity, his courage and his sense of humour. But the work also has striking variety of emphasis. In *Their Finest Hour* he reached heights of passionate eloquence that showed his patriotic fervour at white heat. In *The Grand Alliance* on the other hand, he discloses equally admirable but very different qualities. By 1941

M*

the war had assumed world-wide proportions and great complexity. The new historical material which Churchill handles here is immense, and a lesser man might easily have been overwhelmed by the weight of documents. His mastery of the material, is, however, complete. Skilful selection and compression keep the bulk of the volume within reasonable limits, and the narrative maintains liveliness and impressionistic vigour. While he has polished stateliness in describing the march of events, relief is given in passages that are arresting and even entertaining.

The Churchillian style is famous, and many examples of his inspired phrasing will live as long as the English language continues to be spoken. In his histories, as in his speeches, we find a vast range in his command of English, from noble eloquence to intimate homely words and high-spirited fun. One rare merit he has is his instinctive preference for simple words. Early in the second World War, for example, he sent a memorandum to the heads of the Civil Service Departments urging that jargon should be avoided in official papers, and that the key-note of such documents should be brevity and simplicity. "Let us not", he pleaded, "shrink from the short expressive phrase; even if it is conversational."

On 4 July 1950, the Chesney Gold Medal of the Royal United Service Institution was presented to Sir Winston in the Old Banqueting Hall of Whitehall Palace by Admiral Sir Henry Moore, the Chairman of the Council of the Institution, for his outstanding contributions to service literature and military history. The medal was instituted in 1899 as a memorial to General Sir George Chesney, and has since been awarded at intervals, as suitable occasions arose, to the author of "an original literary work, treating of naval or military science and literature, and which has a bearing on the welfare of the British Empire". It is hard to conceive a more ideal recipient for this honour.

The fourth volume, *The Hinge of Fate*, appeared in 1951, the fifth, *Closing the Ring*, in 1952, and the sixth and final one, *Triumph and Tragedy*, in 1953. In October of the latter year, also, Sir Winston was awarded the Nobel prize for literature because of his brilliant historical writings. He was chosen from candidates from all over the world. The only other historian ever to have had the award was a German, Theodor Mommsen, who received it over half a century earlier for his history of ancient Rome. The prize consists of an illuminated scroll, a gold medal weighing 10 oz., and 175,292 Swedish crowns (about £12,000) payable in sterling.

In his preface to the first volume of the *History of the English-Speaking People,* published in 1956, Sir Winston mentions that twenty years had elapsed since he made the arrangements which resulted in the book. At the outbreak of the war about half a million words had been delivered, but proof-reading had to be set aside when he went to the Admiralty at the beginning of September 1939. Even at the close of hostilities he could not return to the work immediately, being occupied with his war memoirs.

Sir Winston says that his aim in the book is to present a personal view on the processes whereby English-speaking peoples throughout the world have achieved their distinctive position and character. He states that he uses the term "English-speaking peoples" because there is no other that applies both to the inhabitants of the British Isles and to those independent nations who derive their beginnings, their speech, and many of their institutions from England, and who now preserve, nourish, and develop them in their own ways.

The narrative is extremely bold and vivid. In tracing the main course of events, consummate skill is shown in selecting what is truly significant while ignoring pettifogging detail. In consequence, interest is kept at a high pitch, and we move forward rapidly and easily. The great qualities of the author are again apparent: we have on the one hand his shrewd judgment and deep understanding of men and affairs, and on the other his humour, his delight in picturesque incidents, and use of brief caustic comment to drive points home. This magnificent work was completed in 1958.

THE HISTORICAL WORKS OF CHURCHILL
WITH DATES OF PUBLICATION

1898 *The Malakand Field Force* (N.W. Indian Frontier)
1899 *The River War* (Sudan Campaign, 2 Vols.)
1900 *London to Ladysmith via Pretoria* (S. African War, Vol. I)
1900 *Ian Hamilton's March* (Ditto, Vol. II)
1906 *Life of Lord Randolph Churchill.*

1923-29 *The World Crises, 1911-1918, and the Aftermath* (5 Vols.)

1931 *The Eastern Front.*

1933-38 *Marlborough, his Life and Times.*

1948 *The Gathering Storm* (Vol. I of *The Second World War*).

1949 *Their Finest Hour* (Vol. II).

1950 *The Grand Alliance* (Vol. III).

1951 *The Hinge of Fate* (Vol. IV).

1952 *Closing the Ring* (Vol.V).

1953 *Triumph and Tragedy* (Vol. VI).

1956 *The Birth of Britain* (Vol. I of *A History of the English-Speaking Peoples*).

1956 *The New World* (Vol. II).

1957 *The Age of Revolution* (Vol. III).

1958 *The Great Democracies* (Vol. IV).

Works Consulted

DAVID HUME (1711-1776)

A modestly written Autobiography was published in 1774. The excellent standard work, a model of its kind, is the *Life and Correspondence of David Hume*, from the papers bequeathed by his nephew to the Royal Society of Edinburgh, edited by John Hill Burton in 1846. An attractive short life was written by Professor T. H. Huxley, and another in 1931 by J. Y. T. Greig. The historian's Private Correspondence was edited by Dr. Thomas Murray and others, including J. Y. T. Greig, in 1932. Sir Leslie Stephen's *English Thought in the Eighteenth Century* contains valuable information.

ADAM SMITH (1723-1790)

A Life by Dugald Stewart was read as a paper to the Royal Society of Edinburgh in 1793, and was afterwards reprinted as an introduction to Smith's Works. Full and accurate information is given in the *Life of Adam Smith* by John Rae, published in 1895. Rae examined the original records in the possession of the University of Glasgow and elsewhere. Other biographers have included Viscount Haldane, H. C. Macpherson, F. W. Hirst, and W. R. Scott.

OLIVER GOLDSMITH (1728-1774)

The Percy Memoir was first published in 1801. A painstaking Life by James Prior appeared in 1837, but this was largely superseded by a comprehensive work by John Forster, the first edition of which was printed in 1948. Other writers on Goldsmith include Washington Irving, W. Black, Austin Dobson, and S. Gwynn.

EDWARD GIBBON (1737-1794)

Gibbon's *Memoirs of my Life and Writings* were edited by his friend Lord Sheffield in 1796. The *Private Letters of Edward Gibbon* were well edited by R. E. Prothero in 1896. Biographies were written by G. M. Young in 1932 and D. M. Low in 1937. The definitive edition of the *Decline & Fall* is that by Professor J. B. Bury, published in seven volumes between 1896 and 1900. The book had the honour of being bowdlerized by Bowdler himself, with the omission of all irreligious or other objectionable passages.

ROBERT SOUTHEY (1774-1843)

Southey's letters were edited by his son, the Rev. C. C. Southey, in 1849-50, and a further collection of his correspondence was published by his son-in-law, the Rev. J. Wood Warter, in 1856. These give much intimate information. There are also short biographies by C. T. Browne, Professor Dowden, 1874, and J. Simmons, 1945.

W. H. PRESCOTT (1796-1859)

The chief biography is by his friend G. Ticknor, published in 1864. The historian's MSS. and other papers are preserved in the library of the Massachusetts Historical Society. His works were edited by his secretary, J. Foster Kirk, 1884.

LORD MACAULAY (1800-1859)

His nephew, Sir George Otto Trevelyan, published the *Life and Letters of Lord Macaulay* in 1876: a new edition was issued in 1931. Sir Charles Firth's penetrating and scholarly *Commentary on Macaulay's History of England* appeared in 1938.

J. ANTHONY FROUDE (1818-1894)

There is a *Life of Froude* by H. Woodfield Paul, published in 1905. Waldo H. Dunn wrote an account of the Froude-Carlyle controversy in 1930. Other writers on Froude include Professor P. Hume-Brown, Sir Leslie Stephen, and A. Stanton Whitfield.

JOHN RICHARD GREEN (1837-1883)

A Memoir by his wife was written in 1888. His Letters were edited by Sir Leslie Stephen in 1901. There are excellent essays on the historian by James Bryce, published in his *Studies in Contemporary Biography*, and P. Lyttleton Gell.

SIR WINSTON CHURCHILL (1874)

In 1930 Mr. Churchill himself published a fascinating account of his youth under the title of *My Early Life, 1874-1902*. Guy Eden, Robert Sencourt and others have written brief biographies. C. Lewis Broad published his *Winston Churchill, 1874-1945* at the close of the second World War. Malcolm Thomson's *Life and Times of Winston Churchill* also appeared in 1945. Mr. Churchill's biographers have been largely pre-occupied with his political career and war leadership, and have paid little attention to his literary work.

Index

DATE DUE